THE DEMOCRATIC
REPUBLIC OF CONGO

International Peace Academy
Occasional Paper Series

THE DEMOCRATIC
REPUBLIC OF CONGO

Economic Dimensions
of War and Peace

Michael Nest,
with François Grignon
and Emizet F. Kisangani

LYNNE
RIENNER
PUBLISHERS

BOULDER
LONDON

Published in the United States of America in 2006 by
Lynne Rienner Publishers, Inc.
1800 30th Street, Boulder, Colorado 80301
www.rienner.com

and in the United Kingdom by
Lynne Rienner Publishers, Inc.
3 Henrietta Street, Covent Garden, London WC2E 8LU

Library of Congress Cataloging-in-Publication Data
Nest, Michael Wallace.
  The Democratic Republic of Congo : economic dimensions of war and peace /
Michael Nest ; with François Grignon and Emizet F. Kisangani.
     p. cm. — (International Peace Academy occasional paper series)
    Includes bibliographical references and index.
    ISBN 1-58826-233-2 (pbk. : alk. paper)
    1. War—Economic aspects—Congo (Democratic Republic) 2. Congo (Democratic
Republic)—History—1997– 3. Congo (Democratic Republic)—Economic conditions—
1960– 4. Congo (Democratic Republic)—Politics and government—1997– I. Grignon,
François. II. Kisangani, Emizet F. III. Title. IV. Series.
HC955.Z9D458 2006
330.96751—dc22

                                               2005029704

British Cataloguing in Publication Data
A Cataloguing in Publication record for this book
is available from the British Library.

Printed and bound in the United States of America

The paper used in this publication meets the requirements
of the American National Standard for Permanence of
Paper for Printed Library Materials Z39.48-1992.

5 4 3 2 1

Contents

Foreword

Terje Rød-Larsen,
President, International Peace Academy

It is with great pleasure that the International Peace Academy (IPA) presents this book on natural resources and conflict in the Democratic Republic of Congo (DRC). The volume builds upon the work of two distinguished IPA research programs, the Economic Agendas in Civil Wars (EACW) and the Africa Program, both of which have kept a sharp focus on key development and security challenges in Africa. Supported by Oxfam UK and the IPA, the book is the product of a fruitful collaboration between three researchers who have been following for some time the conflict and peace process in the DRC from different vantage points. We are grateful to Michael Nest for coordinating the project and to his coauthors François Grignon and Emizet François Kisangani for their collective efforts to shed greater light on the dynamics of conflict and the opportunities for peace in the DRC.

As the international community continues to grapple with failed peace and recurring civil conflict in various regions, economic forces are increasingly recognized as a primary factor in the logic of contemporary war. In light of recent global experiences with conflict involving natural resources, the role of economic relationships in internal strife cannot be ignored. Indeed, in the context of these wars, illicit networks built around natural resource exploitation leave no member of society unaffected, from national leaders to warlords to ordinary citizens residing in borderlands. In the face of these deeply entrenched economic and political relationships, no lasting peace can be achieved without accounting for the role of economically driven behavior in both conflict resolution and war transformation.

Perhaps no recent conflict better exemplifies the impact of armed contests over natural resources than the tragic war in the Democratic

Republic of Congo. In this wide-ranging and bitter struggle, armed factions seek control over diamonds, coltan, copper, and other resources that provide both the means to continue the war and the object of much of the fighting. This important volume investigates the protracted conflict in the DRC through the lens of natural-resource exploitation in order to understand better the drivers of conflict and thereby what is required for future peace initiatives to succeed. It is hoped that a more thorough understanding of the underlying dynamics involved in resource-rich conflict zones such as the DRC will strengthen current United Nations, regional, and local peacemaking efforts and perhaps prevent economically driven conflicts from developing in the future.

The IPA's support for this project would not have been possible without the assistance of funders who have generously supported the EACW program. The International Peace Academy would like to express its appreciation to the Canadian Department of Foreign Affairs; the Canadian International Development Agency; the governments of Norway, Switzerland, and Sweden; the United Kingdom's Department for International Development; the International Development Research Centre of Canada; the Rockefeller Foundation; and the United Nations Foundation for supporting and encouraging the development of the EACW program and this particular project. In addition we acknowledge, with gratitude, the support of Oxfam UK, which was actively involved in the conceptualization of the project and cofinanced this publication.

Special thanks are due to Karen Ballentine, who led the EACW program in 2001–2004, for her intellectual guidance and support in the initial stages of this project. The project also owes a debt of gratitude to the persistent efforts of IPA vice president Neclâ Tschirgi and publications officer Clara Lee. The IPA is proud to bring this study to the attention of scholars and policymakers in the hope of contributing to a sustainable peace process in the DRC.

Acknowledgments

This is one of a handful of books—an even smaller number of which are in English—dedicated to the deadliest conflict since World War II. I wish to thank the International Peace Academy (IPA) for investing in analyses of the Democratic Republic of Congo and the Congo War and for providing the resources ultimately required to bring this study to its conclusion.

The book was very much a team effort by the authors, with assistance and guidance from the IPA. I would especially like to thank Neclâ Tschirgi for trusting in my abilities to see the book through to its conclusion. Karen Ballentine, a former senior associate of the IPA, provided advice and direction at the beginning of the study that helped sustain it in the years that followed, as did Ciru Mwaura, who also made generous contributions to the book's analysis, not all of which could be included in the final manuscript. Kaysie Studdard, Clara Lee, and Batabiha Bushoki were most helpful and open in their feedback. Many, many thanks to Pierre Englebert, whose careful reading and constructive recommendations greatly improved the original manuscript, and to the anonymous and internal IPA reviewers whose suggestions also helped improve the final product. Lee Ann Fuji and Tatiana Carayannis made timely contributions that saved my neck, and thank you to Ramin for supporting me all the way.

—*Michael Nest*

The Democratic Republic of Congo

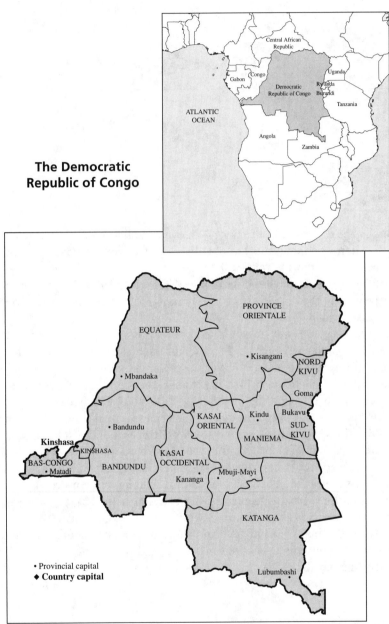

1

Introduction

Since the mid-1990s, economic agendas in civil wars have attracted increasing attention in the analysis of armed conflict. They are the subject of numerous dedicated research projects and are a priority research and policy development issue for a host of organizations.[1] Economic agendas in interstate and civil wars are not new. However, the economic interests of actors engaged in the civil conflicts of the last decade gained particular prominence due to their importance, compared to earlier wars, as motives for continuing hostilities. A key reason for this was the decline in Cold War patrons' financing of conflicts in third countries. Deprived of support from foreign governments, combatants—including state militaries—turned to commercial activities to generate funds to sustain themselves and their military campaigns.[2] The trend toward self-financing on the part of combatants has been greatly facilitated by economic globalization. Globalization has enhanced combatants' ability to export illegally produced goods to markets around the world, as well as to obtain the inputs (such as capital or information) required to produce commodities. Combatant self-financing has also been facilitated by more and more governments embracing neoliberal economic policies that reduce state intervention in trade and state ownership of assets and resources.[3]

Competition over natural resources has also played a prominent role in some of Africa's most intractable conflicts of the 1990s and 2000s, especially in Sierra Leone, Liberia, Angola, and the Democratic Republic of Congo (DRC). Indeed, these four cases have served as exemplars for much of the research on economic agendas in civil conflicts. Yet, while economic interests in these cases have often been accurately described, their precise contribution to the commencement and evolution of conflict and—in particular—peace and reconstruction efforts remains inadequately understood. As a consequence, these conflicts present continuing policy challenges for mediators and peace operations, especially in determining what mix of strategies for conflict resolution and postconflict reconstruction will work, or have worked, best for wars with significant economic dimensions.

This book analyzes the economic dimensions of violent conflict in one case: the Congo War—the civil and international conflict centered on the DRC from August 1998. From the very beginning, neighboring governments were involved in the Congo War, which quickly drew in half a dozen more countries, involved widespread predatory and criminal behavior by all combatants (including the state), and was directly and indirectly responsible for over 3 million deaths.[4] The "official" conflict—the one addressed by the peace process—concluded in June 2003, when the Government of National Unity and Transition, comprising different belligerent groups and civil society representatives, was established.

But the Congo War was preceded by and occurred simultaneously with other local conflicts, especially in eastern DRC where there was outright conflict as early as 1993. Indeed, it is more correct to talk of Congo *wars*. Eighteen months after the official end of hostilities, local conflicts are responsible for an estimated 30,000 new deaths every month.[5] Like the Congo War itself, these local wars have been fundamentally influenced by state behavior, ethnic tensions, and competition over resources—issues that have been inadequately addressed by the official peace process and are unlikely to be addressed by any incoming democratically elected government that takes office after forthcoming elections, likely to be held in late 2006.

In light of ongoing conflict, and given that in late 2004 there was even a formal renewal of hostilities between the DRC government and rebel groups, the overwhelming conclusion must be that the peace process and postconflict reconstruction efforts have not addressed all major grievances or satisfied all major interests. Even in parts of the country where hostilities have ceased, there is a "negative peace" where grievances and structural opportunities for predatory economic behavior remain intact.[6]

As the analyses by the authors demonstrate, the causes of the Congo War are numerous and complex. They include regime survival, "ethnicized" political violence, the weakness of the DRC state (especially an inability to arbitrate land disputes, which was partly caused by state officials' manipulation of such disputes), disputes over citizenship that were also manipulated by state officials and political leaders, and efforts by neighboring governments to force the DRC government to adopt their policy priorities as its own. Scholars and analysts have paid attention to many of these issues, as well as to the *fact* of various actors' economic interests. However, less research and policy attention has focused on how economic interests have limited and shaped peace and reconstruction efforts—both of which are, of course, comparatively recent—and why they have had this effect.

What is clear is that the Congo War, like other wars with similar features, is not merely the product of rebel "greed." Nor is it purely the result of state collapse in a post–Cold War environment of donor withdrawal, political uncertainty, and economic decline. The factors influencing the Congo War have roots that can be traced back through the Mobutu era to patterns of governance first established under Belgian rule. In particular, officials of the state (in all its incarnations—colonial, Mobutuist, Kabilist, and the rebel "parastates" of the Congo War period) have used the same strategies to govern. They have distributed land and rights (especially citizenship) to selected leaders and their ethnically defined communities in order to reduce localized opposition to the state, while simultaneously deepening competition between communities to prevent the emergence of a united opposition; they have also intervened in chiefly succession processes to try to ensure the rise of customary authorities they can manipulate. The DRC state and individual officials also sought to systematically extract revenue for private and institutional purposes. It is under these conditions that ethnic and regional grievances and conflicts over access to natural resources have long flourished.

One of the goals of this book is to recharacterize the Congo War. Far from being a case of "the state collapsed and greedy rebels took advantage," the book recasts the conflict as one where the interests and grievances' of belligerents (including the DRC state, rebel actors, and neighboring governments) are interlinked and historical (i.e., predating the Kabila eras). To this end, the book adopts a political economy approach that focuses on both rebel and state actors.[7] It focuses on economic dimensions because these are inadequately understood in the case of the Congo War. The authors, however, consider political and security interests to be equally important to the conflict (albeit, at different times for each belligerent).

The book proceeds from the observation that international and local efforts to resolve conflicts with significant economic dimensions can be enhanced by a coordinated effort to analyze the role of economic interests in sustaining hostilities during the Congo War. The international community already has a substantial number of tools available to manage conflicts involving natural resources and to use in postconflict reconstruction.[8] In the case of the Congo War, tools have been required to bring rebels into peace negotiations (such as incentives for rebels in the form of a position in the transitional government), to control the predatory and criminal behavior of rebels and state officials (such as the Kimberley Process Certification Scheme for conflict diamonds), and to restructure patterns of governance. Tools already exist for the first two tasks, as evidenced by the examples given. However, their application has been uneven and they have not always worked well nor worked in a complementary fashion. Tools for restructuring patterns of governance—as opposed to improving the *capacity* to govern through institutional strengthening or improving the *quality* of fiscal governance—are yet to be developed in any substantive way. The broader challenge for the international community is to understand what mix of tools is required for any particular conflict or postconflict environment, and the sequence in which they should be applied. This study contributes to that goal by illuminating the tools that have been applied to the Congo War and analyzing where they have and have not worked, and why.

By focusing on a single case, the book complements existing research—especially quantitative studies and theoretical work—by fleshing out our understanding of how economic dimensions have actually shaped specific conflicts. In keeping with a general need for more field-based research on the political economy of armed conflict, "particularly those dynamics that suggest entry points for more effective policy action,"[9] the book also utilizes observations from the field. This occurs most directly in Chapter 4, which is largely based on François Grignon's interviews with participants in the peace process and government officials engaged in brokering the peace and reconstruction efforts.

Throughout the book, the authors analytically distinguish economic motivations from political and security interests. This is partly for the simple purpose of clarity in argument. But it also reflects the overall theme of the book that economic interests were a function of the conflict, rather than vice versa, and should be distinguished from other interests—especially those more salient at the onset of war. However, and notwithstanding their efforts to analytically distinguish economic interests, all three authors agree that economic and other interests are *linked* and that relationships between different interests developed—and evolved—throughout the course of the conflict. Indeed, the links and relationships between different interests are the key reason that peacebuilding and postconflict reconstruction have been so politically and operationally complicated in the DRC and the Great Lakes region. The authors also agree that combatants' reluctance to address economic interests is a key reason for the uneasy trade-off of interests that occurred and that produced a negative peace in some parts of the country and no peace elsewhere. Even if economic interests had been tabled during the peace process, the authors agree that the relationship of these interests to other dimensions of the conflict would have made them difficult—but not impossible—to address.

Author agreement regarding these general themes should not belie disagreement on a core issue. Specifically, and as has occurred in the case of the Congo War peace process, to what degree should peace and reconstruction efforts address political and security interests but leave economic interests either untouched or only superficially addressed in a manner that is only marginally connected to the major thrust of peace efforts? The optimal solution to most conflicts that involve multiple interests is to use a sequenced approach that ensures all interests are eventually tabled and addressed during peace talks. However, given that this approach has not been used to any real effect in the peace process for the Congo War, the question remains an open one that has generated different emphases in each author's analysis.

Chapter 2 traces the historical role of natural resources in shaping economic development and governance in Zaire (now the DRC) and provides background information on the actors, chronology and key events of the Congo War.

Chapter 3 analyzes the roots of the conflict and the motives and strategies of the organizations, enterprises, and individuals involved. It identifies the key challenges posed by the legacies of economic and criminal predation for peace mediation, implementation, and postconflict reconstruction.

Chapter 4 details the various peace processes that preceded and laid the foundation for the transitional government. It analyzes the economic dimensions of these processes, including the relationship between economic interests and political power and how economic interests have shaped belligerents' dispositions toward conflict resolution. It also analyzes the economic interests of the international community and how they have influenced some of the most prominent initiatives created to address the conflict.

Chapter 5 focuses on the challenges created by the war economy for postconflict reconstruction. Drawing on Amartya Sen's "entitlement approach," it identifies the legacies of the war economy and the challenges they pose to peace implementation and reconstruction. It then evaluates reconstruction efforts currently being implemented and identifies specific additional issues that must be addressed if reconstruction is to be truly successful.

Chapter 6 summarizes the key findings of the book and identifies some policy lessons from war and peace in the DRC for more effective approaches to resolving and preventing other conflicts with significant economic dimensions.

Notes

1. The list includes nongovernmental organizations, research institutes, humanitarian and aid organizations, governments, international financial organizations, and the United Nations. For a more detailed description of organizations and the focus of their projects, see David M. Malone and Heiko Nitzschke, "Economic Agendas in Civil Wars: What We Know, What We Need to Know," Discussion Paper No. 2005/07, April 2005, World Institute for Development Economics Research, p. 3.

2. Karen Ballentine and Jake Sherman, eds., *The Political Economy of Armed Conflict: Beyond Greed and Grievance* (Boulder, Colo.: Lynne Rienner, 2003), especially the Introduction and Chapter 2.

3. Ibid., p. 2.

4. International Rescue Committee and the Burnet Institute, "Mortality Rates in the Democratic Republic of Congo: Results from a Nationwide Survey, Conducted April–July 2004" (New York: International Rescue Committee, December 2004).

5. Ibid.

6. Kimberly Maynard, *Healing Communities in Conflict: International Assistance in Complex Emergencies* (New York: Columbia University Press, 1999), Chapter 6.

7. For a discussion of the merits of a political economy approach, and how state- and rebel-centric approaches can influence the explanations that are produced for conflicts, see Charles Cater, "The Political Economy of Conflict and UN Intervention: Rethinking the Critical Cases of Africa," in Ballentine and Sherman, *The Political Economy of Armed Conflict*, pp. 20–29. For a summary of state-centric and rebel-centric approaches, see Karen Ballentine and Heiko Nitzschke, "Beyond Greed and Grievance: Policy Lessons from Studies in the Political Economy of Armed Conflict," an International Peace Academy Policy Report (New York: IPA, October 2003), pp. 3–5.

8. See Ballentine and Nitzschke, "Beyond Greed and Grievance," pp. 12–18.

9. Malone and Nitzschke, "Economic Agendas in Civil Wars," p. 15.

2

Background to the Conflict

Politics and economics in the DRC have always been shaped by the exploitation of its abundant natural resources. Natural resource exploitation lay at the very foundation of the colonial state, generated much of the foreign economic interest in the colony, and shaped its links to foreign governments and global markets.[1] From about 1920 to 1990, one mineral—copper—reigned supreme as the largest source of government revenue and most foreign exchange.[2] The pattern of resource dependence established under Belgian colonial rule, combined with the absence of a democratically accountable regime during the independent era, caused the weakening and fragmentation of the Zairian state. The fragmentation of the state and decline of the formal economy contributed to the rise in an informal and illegal economy that sustained millions of Congolese but contributed to the further weakening of state capacity and authority.

Following independence from Belgium on June 30, 1960, the state structures established under colonialism underwent a rapid collapse, a process in which external actors with interests in the extractive sectors played a major role. The state's territorial control and coercive monopoly was seriously challenged by the Katanga secessionist movement (1960–1963), itself a direct product of collusion between copper-mining interests, the Belgian government, and local political actors that were focused on ensuring continued foreign control of mines in Katanga province.[3] The breakdown of chains of command in the police and military following independence led to a unilateral decision by the Belgian government to return troops to protect Belgians and their property.[4] With the murder of the first democratically elected head of the legislature, Patrice Lumumba, the legitimacy of the nascent state was further

17

threatened. The demise of the Lumumba government was rooted in its perceived threat to the economic interests of Western governments and corporations. Belgian banks and mining corporations had a large stake in the former colony and feared that Lumumba's anticolonial and populist sentiments were evidence of his intention to nationalize the economy—fears that were rooted in their desire to maintain control over Congolese resources.[5] The United States also viewed Lumumba's quickening ties to the Soviet Union as evidence of a pending alignment with the socialist bloc that would extend Soviet and communist influence into Africa, jeopardizing its own.[6]

Some stability was restored by Joseph-Désiré Mobutu, the army commander in chief, following his seizure of power in a coup d'état on November 24, 1965. By 1970, President Mobutu had established a network of patrimonial relations that gave him firm political control. There were few effective competing sources of authority, the army was as disciplined as it ever would be, and early secessionist movements had been crushed.[7] Mobutu's creation of a political network based on patrimonialism, which worked by satisfying the private interests of those involved, led to widespread corruption within the state bureaucracy and contributed to economic malaise.[8] The Mobutu regime tried both to increase its political independence from the foreign-owned corporations that dominated the minerals sector and to increase the taxes it extracted from them. To this end, it nationalized the copper-mining company—renaming it Gécamines—in 1967, and the diamond-mining company, Miba, in 1973, and raised the taxes it levied on these companies.[9] In 1973, it also nationalized plantations and expropriated many businesses owned by non-Congolese that were then handed over to cronies of the regime.[10] These strategies helped to create an indigenous bourgeoisie and to "Africanize" the workforce, but nationalization of the mining industry also unintentionally jeopardized the reliability of mineral rents. By nationalizing Gécamines—the source of between 50 and 80 percent of state revenue from 1960 to 1975[11]—the government exposed itself to greater price fluctuations through its assumption of market risk. This was clearly demonstrated in 1975, when the state collected sharply reduced rents due to the fall in international copper prices. Economic downturn and diminished state revenues had a severe effect on economic and social development. From the mid-1970s, state employees were paid low salaries intermittently, and reduced state expenditure deeply affected state administration and the provision of public goods.[12] Ignoring the fiscal crisis, Mobutu continued directing ever larger proportions of state revenues toward the presidency and the maintenance of patrimonial systems of rule, and away from economic investment or public goods provision.[13]

By the 1990s, the Zairian state had become highly fragmented, with sharp variations in capacity and presence across the country. Along with Liberia, Angola, Somalia, Sierra Leone, and Afghanistan, scholars identified it as a new type of "fragmented" or "failed" state, which featured "loss of control over and fragmentation of the instruments of physical coercion," a "failure to sustain physical control over the territory and to command popular allegiance," and a reduced ability to collect taxes that "greatly weaken(ed) the revenue base of the state."[14] The Zairian state was further weakened by a series of events in the early 1990s. First, copper production collapsed in September 1990, when the roof of the Kamoto mine—Gécamines' star performer—caved in, causing Gécamines' total production to drop 90 percent between 1989 and 1993.[15] Second, former Cold War patrons withdrew financial and diplomatic support in the early 1990s, following a reassessment of their relations with third world dictators. Third, in response to domestic and foreign pressure to reform in the wake of transitions to democracy elsewhere in Africa and Europe, Mobutu tried to stage-manage a transition by announcing the end of one-party rule in April 1990 and a commitment to reform. His resolve was soon tested by students at the Université de Lubumbashi, who demonstrated against his regime. Concerned that such overt activism might spread across the country, he ordered in his special guard, which massacred 100 students.[16] Pressure for reform continued to mount and in 1991, Mobutu agreed to a multiparty Sovereign National Conference (SNC) to focus on the issue of political liberalization. The SNC quickly evolved into broad national debate with elements of a "truth and reconciliation" process, including an outpouring of criticism against Mobutu and his regime.[17] Mobutu tried to undermine the SNC by ignoring its election of a new (anti-Mobutu) prime minister, as well as by using soldiers to prevent the legislature from assembling. Fourth, from 1990 to 1993, unpaid soldiers engaged in widespread looting of private property.[18] Mobutu's attempts to undermine the popular SNC, the Université de Lubumbashi massacre, and the virtual cessation of state financing of public services and public salaries destroyed any remaining legitimacy of the Mobutu regime, the military, and the state elite.

The Zairian political economy was additionally reconfigured as a result of a boom in the informal economy, especially involving primary commodities, trade, transport, and construction.[19] Together with social networks involving family, extended clans, and civil society organizations (especially churches), the informal economy enabled tens of millions of Congolese to survive despite crumbling state services and economic collapse. Finally, as in other countries that have experienced similar breakdowns of law and order, Zaire saw the rise of regional strongmen or "warlords" who levied taxes from producers and the public and established near monopolies on the buying, selling, and illegal export of commodities, especially coffee, gold, and diamonds.[20] These warlords, invariably allies of Mobutu, derived power from their connections to him and their control of coercive forces. Mobutu gave them a free economic rein on the condition that they did not cross the threshold of outright political opposition to his rule.[21]

Mobutu's final demise was linked to the Rwandan genocide in 1994, when nearly a million Tutsis and moderate Hutus were slaughtered over three months. In the wake of the genocide, over a million Rwandans fled to Zaire, including armed Interahamwe *génocidaires*, who committed most of the killings; officials from the Hutu Power organization who masterminded the genocide; and Hutus frightened that the Tutsi-led forces that halted the genocide and overthrew the Hutu-dominated government would kill them.[22] Refugee camps were established in the Kivus, and occupants were fed by the UN High Commissioner for Refugees (UNHCR) and international donor organizations. But neither Mobutu, the Forces Armées Zairoises (FAZ), nor the United Nations had any authority within the camps. These conditions enabled Hutu Power and Interahamwe to reorganize—indeed, they controlled the camps—and launch attacks across the border into Rwanda.[23]

The decisive factor in Mobutu's downfall was the decision by three neighboring governments to support a military campaign against his regime. In the case of the Rwandan government, which sought the destruction of Interahamwe and Hutu Power organizations located in Zaire, this was explicitly linked to the genocide. In the case of the Ugandan and Angolan governments, the primary motivation was their desire to get rid of Mobutu.

The effect of the genocide and its aftermath on the DRC has been to heighten long-standing tensions in the provinces of North Kivu and South Kivu over land, regional political dominance, and access to state-distributed resources (including citizenship). Central to these issues are disputes between *autochtones* ("indigenous" Congolese) and Kinyarwanda speakers (people who trace their ancestry and language to Rwanda), and the relationships of both these groups to the DRC state. Kinyarwanda speakers are divided into Banyamulenge and

Banyarwanda—communities that migrated from Rwanda to the Kivus in the nineteenth century and the 1960s, respectively.[24] Members of these communities further identify as Hutu and Tutsi.

These cleavages and tensions have made the Kivus "notoriously difficult to govern,"[25] particularly as society and politics have been profoundly influenced by events in neighboring Rwanda and Burundi—events over which DRC officials have had virtually no control.[26] In their attempt to govern the region, officials of the state have always adopted the same strategies: distributing resources to selected local leaders and communities in order to reduce opposition to the state while simultaneously deepening competition between communities to prevent the emergence of a united local opposition, and intervening in chiefly succession processes to try to ensure the rise of chiefs they can manipulate. The latter were groomed to be intermediaries between the state and the local population. As noted by Denis Tull, the continuity of this pattern over the past century "bespeaks a definite path dependency, with a stunning lack of institutional innovation."[27]

Land in the Kivus has become more valuable over the past century as the amount available to the local population has decreased. First, the colonial state appropriated enormous tracts of land from customary chiefs and gave it to white settlers and mining companies. Instead of being returned to their customary owners following independence, these lands were held by the state and strategically distributed as a resource. Second, population growth coupled with regular influxes of people from Rwanda and Burundi resulted in greater competition for the holdings that were available.

Because the key determinant of access to state-owned lands was citizenship, these two resources became linked. During the Mobutu era, the government introduced a decree in 1972 that made Banyamulenge and Banyarwanda citizens, only to introduce a law in 1981 that revoked citizenship for Banyarwanda and even some Banyamulenge (citizens' ancestry in Congo had to be traceable to 1885); then, in 1991, the SNC reaffirmed the 1981 law.[28]

The 1972 decree followed Tutsi-organized genocidal violence in Burundi that targeted Hutus.[29] Fleeing Hutus entered the Kivus causing the local population to see itself "as an imperiled 'indigenous' majority," and causing Banyamulenge and Banyarwanda to seek citizenship in an attempt to get this majority to distinguish between Kinyarwanda speakers and the newcomers.[30] The decree expanded the rights of Kinyarwanda speakers, once largely restricted to being traders and tenant farmers, by enabling them to buy land, vote, stand for political office, and work in the bureaucracy. As part of his strategy for control of the region, Mobutu also distributed land expropriated from Belgian settlers to Banyamulenge and Banyarwanda, recruited them into the civil service, and promoted elected officials to senior ranks of his regime. These rights and subsequent opportunities allayed many Kinyarwanda speakers' fears about being a minority with nowhere else to go. The revocation of citizenship in 1981 and the reaffirmation of this law in 1991 understandably caused the Banyamulenge and Banyarwanda communities great consternation and insecurity even before the Rwandan genocide in 1994.

Autochthonous groups had also been alarmed at the course of these developments, although at different times and for different reasons. They interpreted the 1972 decree and its creation of opportunities for Kinyarwanda speakers as evidence of "growing Tutsi influence within the state apparatus" and resented the expanding number and size of Banyamulenge- and Banyarwanda-controlled landholdings.[31] Most customary chiefs were unable to similarly expand their landholdings (unless they could afford freehold title), because they were restricted to their communities' customary lands and constrained by inheritance patterns that resulted in land being divided into ever smaller parcels among expanding communities. Autochthonous chiefs and leaders supported the 1981 law in the hope that it would restore their economic and political preeminence, and Mobutu, judging that he may have alienated *autochtones* too far and needing the support of Kinyarwanda supporters less than he did in 1972, approved it. When Mobutu began to lose his grip on politics in 1991—especially the agenda of the SNC—well-organized and outspoken autochthonous leaders pushed through the SNC's resolution on citizenship.[32]

The Rwandan genocide and eventual military victory by the Tutsi-dominated Rwandan Patriotic Front (RPF) over Hutu Power and its militias, brought these tensions involving land, citizenship, and ethnicity in the Kivus yet again to a head. Indigenous Congolese felt imperiled at the latest in-flow of Kinyarwanda speakers (in this case, Hutus) and were suspicious of both the links between the RPF and Banyamulenge and Banyarwanda communities (from which the RPF had recruited soldiers) and the RPF's intentions vis-à-vis the DRC. Of course, Banyamulenge and Banyarwanda felt acutely threatened by the *géno-cidaires* in their midst and the rising political mobilization around ethnicity. They were also increasingly identified as Tutsi (i.e., lumped together with Rwandan Tutsis) and suffered armed attacks on their communities. Using their existing links to the new Tutsi-dominated

Rwandan government, these communities sought, and received, weapons and training from the RPF.

In late 1996, in response to ongoing attacks originating from refugee camps, the renamed Rwandan Patriotic Army (RPA) entered Zaire to disperse refugees from the camps and to capture and kill *génocidaires*—a campaign that had great success. The RPA was soon joined by the Uganda People's Defence Force (UPDF). The president of Uganda, Yoweri Museveni, was keen to get rid of Mobutu because he had allowed Ugandan opposition groups to launch attacks on the UPDF from Zairian territory.[33] Museveni was also a close ally of senior Rwandan leaders, most of whom had served in the UDPF while in exile from Rwanda. Together, the RPA and UPDF organized the Alliance des Forces Démocratiques pour la Libération du Congo-Zaire (AFDL), which led the campaign against Hutu militias and FAZ troops that got in the way.[34]

At the heart of the AFDL were members of the Banyamulenge and Banyarwanda communities who were anti-Mobutu and wanted to stop attacks on their communities. Other domestic groups also joined the campaign, especially as it achieved greater military success. The head of one of these groups, Laurent-Désiré Kabila (hereafter, Laurent Kabila), was chosen to head the AFDL because he brought the alliance "credibility among the wider Congolese population. As a member of the Baluba tribe in the southwest Katanga province, he had consistently opposed Mobutu . . . and was therefore considered untainted."[35] The campaign gained more external support from the Angolan government, which had a long-standing grudge against Mobutu because he had allowed União Nacional para a Independência Total de Angola (UNITA) forces to operate bases in the DRC. The bases functioned as a conduit for weapons and diamonds and helped sustained UNITA in its war against the Angolan government.

Meeting little resistance to its attacks on the refugee camps and no opposition from FAZ soldiers who deserted, the AFDL advanced north, south, and west. After an eight-month campaign, the AFDL forces entered Kinshasa on May 17, 1997; Mobutu had fled shortly before and died in exile in Morocco in September. Laurent Kabila declared himself president, and Zaire was renamed the Democratic Republic of Congo (DRC).

Integral to the success of the AFDL was the revenue generated from mineral commodities. With military capacity but few cash resources at the start of its campaign, the AFDL set about selling state-controlled assets—assets it did not yet control—in exchange for cash. Michael L. Ross describes this exchange as part of a new "booty futures" market and argues that the proliferation of civil wars in Africa is linked to the growth of such markets. Booty futures enable aspiring rebel groups that stand a chance of obtaining valuable resources in combat to "sell off the future right to exploit the resources it hopes to capture, either to a foreign firm or a neighboring government."[36] Booty futures may consequently prolong hostilities and make natural resource exploitation central to belligerents' strategies and interests even if it initially was not. In the DRC case, the sale of booty futures occurred in 1996 and 1997 when the AFDL raised funds by selling future production of cobalt, copper, and zinc to private foreign companies.[37]

A Second War Breaks Out

The origins of the Congo War—as distinct from the war to overthrow the Mobutu regime—can be traced to two discrete factors. First, Laurent Kabila sought greater autonomy from the Rwandan and Ugandan patrons who put him in power, a development that displeased Rwandan and Ugandan officials. Second, there was a large number of disgruntled and powerful Congolese who opposed Laurent Kabila and were unhappy with the pace and extent of the government's economic and political reforms.[38] The existence of this domestic base facilitated efforts by the Rwandan government, and later the Ugandan government, to build a political and military campaign against the DRC government.

Prior to the outbreak of the Congo War in August 1998, the fifteen-month period from May 1997 was a time of political, social, and economic reconfiguration. The political goal of the AFDL regime in Kinshasa was to increase revenues and rebuild state capacity to consolidate its authority and control over coercive forces throughout the country, as well as to provide public goods to increase its legitimacy in the eyes of the population.[39] Yet the AFDL coalition experienced domestic criticism and internal divisions from its earliest days. In particular, non-Tutsi Congolese resented the prominence of Banyamulenge, Banyarwanda, and Rwandan advisers in senior positions and thought their presence compromised DRC sovereignty and blocked their personal career aspirations.[40] These divisions had both nationalistic and ethnicist (racist) elements. Then, in mid-1998, Laurent Kabila became increasingly independent and refused to cooperate with the Rwandan government in arresting the Interahamwe responsible for the genocide or in disarming Hutu Power militias that continued to launch attacks on Rwanda. This was an astonishing turnaround given that these forces had supported Mobutu and that Laurent Kabila's own troops had assisted the RPA in attacking Hutu groups fleeing the AFDL in 1997.[41] Laurent Kabila asked Rwandan forces to leave in July 1998, which they eventually did. The AFDL regime's relations with the Ugandan government also soured when senior Congolese officials accused Uganda officials of profit seeking.[42]

Tensions within the AFDL erupted into clashes between Tutsi and non-Tutsi troops in barracks in Kinshasa, Bukavu, and Goma on August 2, 1998.[43] The commander of the Goma-based Tenth Battalion of the Armée Nationale Congolaise renounced his allegiance to President Kabila on the local Voice of the People radio station, shortly followed by a similar declaration by the Bukavu-based 222nd Brigade.[44] The following day, military leaders of the mutiny announced that they were in military control of Goma, Bukavu, Uvira, and other eastern towns. In Kinshasa, Banyamulenge, Banyarwanda, and Rwandans began to flee the city fearing retribution. Then on August 4, the rebels, backed by RPA forces, commandeered a Congolese cargo plane in Goma and flew 1,200 miles to the Kitona military base on the Atlantic coast, where they launched a military campaign aimed at occupying Kinshasa and removing Laurent Kabila from power.[45] The hitherto military campaign developed a public political profile on August 15, when Bizima Karaha, a Banyamulenge former foreign minister under Laurent Kabila, announced that Congolese opposition leaders had formed the Congolese Democratic Movement (later to become the Rassemblement Congolais pour la Démocratie—RCD) to replace Kabila's government.

Following a fact-finding mission to the DRC by the Southern African Development Community (SADC), an organization the DRC joined in 1997, the Zimbabwe Defence Forces (ZDF) and the Angolan army entered the war on August 20, on the side of the DRC government and defeated the rebel and RPA forces advancing on Kinshasa.[46] However, from their strongholds in eastern DRC, Rwandan and Ugandan forces—the UPDF entered the conflict against the government in late August, after the ZDF had intervened on behalf of the DRC government—advanced westward toward the diamond fields of East Kasai and south toward the copper mines of Katanga.

Simultaneously, a new rebel group—Mouvement pour la Libération du Congo (MLC)—advanced west and south along the Congo River toward Kinshasa from its strongholds in Orientale and Equateur provinces. The MLC is headed by Jean-Pierre Bemba and run by a coalition of wealthy private entrepreneurs and some former high-ranking figures from the Mobutu era—a feature common to other rebel

groups and even the Laurent Kabila government, which invited some
Mobutuists into the fold after the break with Rwanda.

By mid-1999, the war reached a military stalemate after the
Zimbabwean and Angolan governments poured in troops to support
Laurent Kabila. Several battles occurred in 2000, but they had little
impact in terms of exchanges of territory. A fractured frontline stretched
from roughly the northwest to the southeast of the country, splitting the
country in two. Progovernment forces were concentrated in the west and
south, and antigovernment forces were concentrated in the east and
north.

Progovernment forces focused on assisting the DRC government's
Forces Armées Congolaises (FAC). The major foreign allies were the
ZDF and Angolan army, although the latter reduced its presence as the
war wore on. Troops from the militaries of Namibia, Chad, Eritrea, and
Sudan also assisted the DRC government early in the conflict but mostly
withdrew after a few months. Other foreign forces to ally themselves
with the DRC government were two Burundian Hutu militias that were
involved in their own conflict in Burundi with the Tutsi-dominated
Burundian army. Domestic, Congolese, progovernment forces included
Mai Mai militias, which were located deep within rebel-held territory
and cooperated with the FAC while simultaneously pursuing their own
local agendas. In addition, Interahamwe forces and many former members of the Forces Armées Rwandaises (FAR) that had remained in the
DRC after escaping the RPA's assault on refugee camps in 1996 also
assisted the DRC government. Many Interahamwe and ex-FAR joined
the Force Démocratique de Libération du Rwanda (FDLR), which was
formed by exiled Rwandans in 2000 with the objective of overthrowing
the Tutsi-dominated Rwandan government.

On the antigovernment side, the main Congolese groups were the
RCD and MLC. Both groups sought a share of government, albeit by
using force to demonstrate they were a power to be reckoned with.
These rebel groups were militarily and organizationally linked to the
RPA and UPDF, which were the chief foreign antigovernment forces
during the Congo War. The RCD was very closely allied to the RPA, less
so to the UPDF. The MLC, on the other hand, received military support
from the UPDF but had much looser ties to the RPA. The Burundian
army—which gave some support to the RCD—and UNITA forces also
played minor roles.

Relations within rebel groups, and between them and their foreign
backers, were fractious (see Chapter 4 for an expanded analysis of relations between rebel groups). In 1999, disagreement between the UPDF

and RPA over who should lead the RCD resulted in the group splitting into two factions: RCD-Goma and RCD-ML (-Mouvement de Libération). The latter was aligned with Kampala and relocated to Kisangani, then in the hands of the UPDF. Following clashes in the first half of 2000 between the UPDF and RPA over control of the local diamond industry in Kisangani, the RCD-ML moved its headquarters once again—this time to Bunia, closer to the Ugandan border. The RCD-ML also briefly merged with the MLC to form the Front de Libération du Congo (FLC) headed by Jean-Pierre Bemba. However, the FLC soon split along the lines of the original parties following acrimony over Bemba's attempt to extract high taxes from areas under the RCD-ML's control and bring these areas under the direct military control of the MLC. These coalitions resulted in three broad zones of military influence in territory occupied by antigovernment forces: a MLC/Ugandan zone in north and northwestern DRC, a RCD-ML/Ugandan zone in the northeast, and a RCD-Goma/Rwanda zone in central-eastern DRC.

Conclusion

For such a politically complicated conflict, the Congo War has been punctuated by remarkably few major political developments. Those that have occurred, however, changed the course of the conflict. The first was the mass entry into the conflict of foreign militaries. The second was the RCD's split into two major factions, which resulted in the creation of two rebel-held territorial zones in eastern DRC (in addition to the MLC's northern zone). The third development was the assassination of Laurent Kabila on January 16, 2001, and his replacement by his son, Joseph. Joseph Kabila's ascendancy to the presidency saw an immediate improvement in the DRC government's relations with international financial institutions (IFIs) and Western governments, as well as movement on peace talks. The fourth development was the formation of a Government of National Unity and Transition ("transitional government") on June 30, 2003, which marked the official end to the formal conflict.

These political events mark a critical phase in the history of the DRC, akin to the crisis period of the Lumumba government when many paths seemed possible and fateful choices were made. The involvement of armies, militias, and entrepreneurs from neighboring countries in both the growing conflagration and the development of a war economy has also been a watershed in international and commercial relations on the continent. Never has such a range of African actors, especially governments, sought to shape the political economy of another African state to such a degree.

Notes

1. See, for example, Raymond Leslie Buell, *The Native Problem in Africa*, vol. 2 (New York: Macmillan, 1928); Adam Hochschild, *King Leopold's Ghost: A Story of Greed, Terror, and Heroism in Colonial Africa* (Boston: Houghton Mifflin, 1998).
2. Crawford Young and Thomas Turner, *The Rise and Decline of the Zairian State* (Madison: University of Wisconsin Press, 1985); Michael Nest, "The Evolution of a Fragmented State: The Case of the Democratic Republic of Congo" (Ph.D. diss., New York University, May 2002).
3. For an expanded history, see Crawford Young, *Politics in the Congo: Decolonization and Independence* (Princeton: Princeton University Press, 1965); Ludo De Witte, *The Assassination of Lumumba* (London: Verso, 2001).
4. Young, *Politics in the Congo*.
5. De Witte, *The Assassination of Lumumba*.
6. Michael G. Schatzberg, *Mobutu or Chaos? The United States and Zaire, 1960–1990* (Philadelphia: University Press of America, 1991).
7. Young and Turner, *The Rise and Decline of the Zairian State*.
8. Thomas Callaghy, *The State-Society Struggle: Zaire in Comparative Perspective* (New York: Columbia University Press, 1984).
9. Young and Turner, *The Rise and Decline of the Zairian State*.
10. Ibid.; Michael G. Schatzberg, *Politics and Class in Zaire: Bureaucracy, Business, and Beer in Lisala* (New York: Africana Publishing, 1980).
11. Nest, "The Evolution of a Fragmented State" (see Fig. 1.6, p. 53).
12. Ibid., pp. 51–52.
13. William Reno, "Sovereignty and Personal Rule in Zaire," *African Studies Quarterly* 1, no. 3, available online at www.africa.ufl.edu/asq/v1/3/4.htm.
14. Mary Kaldor, *New and Old Wars: Organized Violence in a Global Era* (Stanford, Calif.: Stanford University Press, 1999), p. 52.
15. Author's confidential interview with mining company official, Lubumbashi, 1999; U.S. Geological Survey, *Minerals Yearbook* (Washington, D.C.: U.S. Bureau of Mines, 1991).
16. Agence France-Presse, "Lubumbashi Massacres Kill 100," May 22, 1991.
17. Mahmood Mamdani, *When Victims Become Killers: Colonialism, Nativism, and the Genocide in Rwanda* (Princeton: Princeton University Press, 2001), pp. 245–247.
18. Jean-Claude Willame, *Zaire: Predicament and Prospects* (New York: Minority Rights Group, 1997).
19. Janet MacGaffey, with Vwakyanakazi Mukohya, *The Real Economy of*

Zaire: The Contribution of Smuggling and Other Unofficial Activities to National Wealth (Philadelphia: University of Pennsylvania Press, 1991).

20. For the rise of warlords in Zaire, see Reno, *Sovereignty and Personal Rule in Zaire*. For other countries, see Mark Duffield, "Post-modern Conflict: Warlords, Post-adjustment States and Private Protection," *Civil Wars* 1, no. 1 (spring 1998): 65–102; William Reno, *Warlord Politics and African States* (Boulder, Colo.: Lynne Rienner, 1998); Kaldor, *New and Old Wars*.

21. An example of a warlord who crossed this threshold is Kyungu wa Kumwanza, governor of Katanga in the early 1990s and a political ally of Mobutu. Kyungu collaborated with Mobutu's special presidential guard to steal cobalt from Gécamines and illegally ship it to Zambia where it was sold. Kyungu became too powerful and was arrested in 1995 for allegedly importing arms for a secession attempt. Thomas Callaghy, "From Reshaping to Resizing a Failing State? The Case of the Congo/Zaire" (manuscript, 1998).

22. These fears were realized when several hundred thousand Rwandans—some, but not all, of whom were *génocidaires* and former members of Hutu Power—were killed by Rwandan troops and the alliance of forces that eventually overthrew Mobutu. See Amnesty International, *Deadly Alliances in Congolese Forests* (New York: Amnesty International, 1997).

23. Philip Gourevitch, *We Wish to Inform You That Tomorrow We Will Be Killed with Our Families: Stories from Rwanda* (New York: Harper, 1998).

24. Jean-Claude Willame, *Banyarwanda et Banyamulenge: Violences ethniques et gestion de l'identitaire au Kivu* (Brussels: Institut africain–CEDAF; Paris: L'Harmattan, 1997).

25. Denis M. Tull, "A Reconfiguration of Political Order? The State of the State in North Kivu (DR Congo)," *African Affairs* 102, no. 408 (2003): 431.

26. These events, especially those resulting in population flows into the DRC, have contributed to North Kivu and South Kivu having distinct histories and politics. Migrations from Rwanda and Burundi to the Kivus have varied in their cause, timing, direction, ethnic composition, and size and have had a subsequently varying impact throughout eastern DRC.

27. Tull, "A Reconfiguration of Political Order?" p. 446.

28. See Mamdani, *When Victims Become Killers*; Willame, *Banyarwanda et Banyamulenge*.

29. For a brief account of this genocide, see René Lemarchand, "Genocide in the Great Lakes: Which Genocide? Whose Genocide," *African Studies Review* 41, no. 1 (1998).

30. Mamdani, *When Victims Become Killers*, p. 243.

31. Ibid.

32. Ibid., pp. 245–247.

33. John F. Clark, "Explaining Ugandan Intervention in Congo: Evidence and Interpretations," *Journal of Modern African Studies* 39, no. 2 (2001): 261–287.

34. For a detailed description of the AFDL and its evolution, see Gauthier De Villers, Jean-Claude Willame, Jean Omasombo Tshonda, and Eric Kennes, *République démocratique du Congo: Chronique politique de l'entre-deux-guerres, Octobre 1996–Juillet 1998*, Cahiers Africains 35–36 (Tervuren, Belgium: Institut africain–CEDAF, 1998).

35. David Shearer, "Africa's Great War," *Survival* 41, no. 2 (summer 1999): 92.

36. Michael L. Ross, "Booty Futures: Africa's Civil Wars and the Futures Market for Natural Resources," paper presented at the American Political Science Association annual conference, 2002, p. 8.

37. François Misser, "Fools Rush In . . . and Out?" *African Business*, March 1998, pp. 27–28.

38. Shearer, "Africa's Great War," p. 93.

39. Nest, "The Evolution of a Fragmented State," especially Chapter 5.

40. Callaghy, *From Reshaping to Resizing a Failing State?* p. 20.

41. Shearer, "Africa's Great War"; Amnesty International, *Deadly Alliances in Congolese Forests*, pp. 38–40.

42. Clark, "Explaining Ugandan Intervention in Congo."

43. In December 2004, it was again tensions between Tutsi and non-Tutsi that threatened the foundation of the government (in this case, the transitional government). See International Crisis Group, *Back to the Brink in the Congo*, Africa Briefing No. 21 (Nairobi: ICG, December 17, 2004).

44. CNN.com, "Kinshasa Under Curfew as Congo Army Revolts Against Kabila," August 3, 1998.

45. CNN.com, "Congo Leader Kabila Vows to Crush Rebels," August 4, 1998.

46. Economist Intelligence Unit, *DRC Country Report*, November 1998.

47. Clark, "Explaining Ugandan Intervention in Congo."

48. Tatiana Carayannis, "Rebels with a Cause? A Study of the Mouvement de Libération du Congo," paper delivered at the Africa Studies Association annual conference, Washington, D.C., December 5–8, 2002.

3

The Political Economy
of the Congo War

The Congo War has been described as a new "scramble for Africa," given its apparent similarities to European powers' scramble to colonize and exploit the continent in the late nineteenth century.[1] Networks largely engaged in taxing trade and producing primary commodities were a feature of the wartime political economy, as were battles for control over mineral deposits. Congolese politicians, bureaucrats, and militias, as well as intervening military forces, were all seemingly motivated by the profits they could extract from the DRC's natural resources. The evidence suggests, however, that these actors' *initial* motives in entering the war were not economic. Rather, they were a complex and evolving combination of regime security, concern at preventing ethnic-based harassment and killings, grievances related to access to land and citizenship rights, domestic political leaders' interest in obtaining a "seat at the table" of a new post-Mobutu regime, and the desire by neighboring governments to maintain their political dominance within the region. While economic agendas became a prominent part of the conflict, they emerged as a function of war; war did not occur as a result of economic interests.

The specific origins of the Congo War can be traced to President Laurent Kabila's desire to become more independent from his Rwandan and Ugandan sponsors, as well as domestic discontent with the extent and pace of the government's political and economic reforms. Economic interests became significant for many actors in the war when they were unable to achieve an early victory and had to finance ongoing military campaigns. In addition, various individuals and organizations became cognizant of the profit-making opportunities available to them from their presence in the DRC and their links to foreign militaries deployed there.

The emergence of economic interests transformed the war and, combined with continuing political interests, resulted in a predatory, exploitative and multiwar "complex." These Congo wars merged interstate conflict and civil war—between the DRC government and domestic groups, as well as a spillover civil war between the RPA and Interahamwe—with local disputes that became integrated into the strategies and campaigns of more powerful military actors. Local conflicts resulted in intense fighting (involving rebel, Mai Mai, RPA, and UPDF forces) that occurred for a variety of military, political, and economic reasons, including ethnically targeted killings, revenge for prior killings, theft of goods and livestock, and disputes (motivated by both strategic and economic reasons) over the control of land and certain towns. Belligerents in all these conflicts integrated their strategies with those of other types of actors (including militaries, foreign governments, and private firms) in order to more efficiently exploit economic opportunities. These multilevel, multiactor, networks crossed many borders, and their development further regionalized and internationalized the DRC war economy and facilitated the penetration of criminal elements into the DRC.

Congolese actors were an integral and essential part of the regional commercial networks that became a feature of the Congo War. They were not always equal partners in their relationship with foreign, especially military, actors. However, Congolese actors were also not merely manipulated or coerced by foreigners—they, themselves, sometimes manipulated foreigners.

Why did economic interests become central to the conflict and why did these interests shape the course and character of the war the way they did? This chapter answers these questions by analyzing the emergence of a war economy and the effect on combatants of the conditions created by the conflict. It concludes by describing the challenges created by the war economy for peace and postconflict reconstruction.

The Emergence of a War Economy

The Congo War has transformed the DRC economy and contributed to the preexisting trend toward decline of the formal economy. The conflict also disrupted the informal social and economic networks that had enabled Congolese to survive. Many Congolese slid further into poverty, and by 2000, per capita income was 25 percent of 1970 levels (see Figure 3.1).

Prewar patterns of trade were reconfigured and economic activity

Figure 3.1 Change in GDP and GDP per capita, 1960–2000 (1995 = 100)

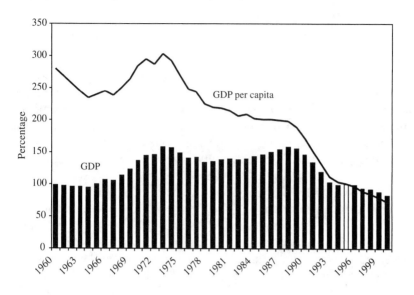

Source: Bernardin Akitoby and Matthias Cinyabuguma, *Sources of Growth in the Democratic Republic of Congo: A Cointegration Approach*, Working Paper WP/04/114 (Washington, D.C.: International Monetary Fund, July 2004). Data was sourced from the IMF webpage: www.imf.org/external/pubs/ft/wp/2004/wp04114.pdf.

became concentrated in certain sectors as other sectors declined. As in other conflicted countries, insecurity and the high cost of doing business caused commercial actors operating in the DRC to seek quick returns from products that were relatively easy to produce and transport.[2] Agriculture was especially affected as insecurity prevented smallholders from visiting their fields.[3] Hostilities halted commerce along the Congo River (the economic lifeblood of millions of people in Equateur and Orientale provinces), and entrepreneurs were cut off from suppliers and markets in other parts of the country. The government's fledgling programs to facilitate economic growth, such as agricultural extension and infrastructure rehabilitation, also came to a halt. However, in a reversal of the trend of foreign disinvestment that had developed since nationalization programs in the late 1960s and early 1970s, there was an *increase* in foreign involvement in the formal economy, mainly due to economic liberalization policies adopted by the Kabila governments that permitted foreign investments and joint ventures.[4]

Broad economic changes during the Congo War are difficult to capture accurately because data cover only the formal sector. The data that
are available indicate different trends for different subsectors (see Figure
3.2). The only clear trend is that of overall decline in agricultural output,
which provided 50 percent of gross national product and a livelihood for
most Congolese. The rise in trade and commerce in 2000 and 2001 probably reflects the consolidation of trade monopolies by various military
actors as the conflict continued, as well as a stalemate on the battlefield
(there is evidence that the important battles that occurred earlier in the
conflict also had a negative effect on commerce and investment[5]). Output
in mining fluctuated. The peak in 1998 may represent a surge in production that occurred *before* the outbreak of conflict in August of that year,
followed by a sharp decline when investors fled as fighting occurred
close to the diamond areas of East Kasai and there was an advance by
rebel troops on the mining areas of Katanga. The causes of the second
peak for mining output in 2000 are unclear. Possibly it is the result of
increased output as the natural resource production and marketing networks controlled by military actors became better developed.

Figure 3.2 Change in Output for Selected Subsectors, 1996–2001

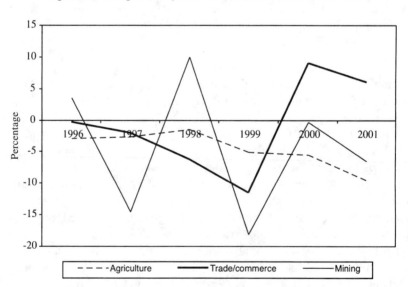

Source: International Monetary Fund, *Democratic Republic of Congo: Request for a
Three-Year Arrangement Under the Poverty Reduction and Growth Facility and for the First
Annual Program—Staff Report*, Country Report No. 02/145 (Washington, D.C.: IMF, July
2002), table 4.

In a pattern common to Sierra Leone, Angola, Cambodia, and Afghanistan during their civil wars, commerce in the DRC became concentrated in "border towns and internal trading gateways" and the trunk routes and airports that linked them.[6] These were the safest places to do business. In the government zone, there was variation in the degree of extortion by military personnel in such enclaves and along the trading routes that connected them, although in general such behavior became more common as the conflict progressed and FAC troops were increasingly not paid.[7] In territory controlled by antigovernment forces, extortion was widespread and there was also some legal trade where civilians were paid for labor or goods.[8]

The resulting insecurity in eastern DRC had a devastating effect on rural agricultural communities dependent on selling crops or subsistence production. Rape, murder, assault, and looting by Interahamwe, Mai Mai, and antigovernment forces made villagers afraid to travel to their fields. This has caused a sharp reduction in agricultural output and caused food scarcity that has contributed to poor health and high mortality rates (the impact of the conflict on subsistence agriculture is analyzed in more detail in Chapter 5).[9]

In a development reminiscent of the colonial era, the economy has also become almost exclusively geared toward the export of primary commodities. This has occurred as the result of a new set of actors that were previously insignificant players in the DRC economy: the commercial units of foreign military forces; the party and military elites of Rwanda, Uganda, and Zimbabwe; and private entrepreneurs from Zimbabwe who, historically, had little interest in the DRC.

There has also developed a substantial criminal component, a trend that was facilitated by the state's weak capacity, the large and illegal informal economy that existed prior to the war, and belligerents' use of coercion as a factor in production.[10] In addition, insecurity and the high cost of doing business caused commercial actors to seek quick returns from activities that required minimal investment, such as taxing trade and producing certain primary commodities, especially minerals.[11] As these activities became better organized and their profitability more apparent, their continuation became an incentive for belligerents to remain armed and deployed.

Economic Agendas as a Function of War

The evidence suggests that actors in the Congo War were initially motivated by political and military interests but that this set of interests has evolved to include a significant economic component, particularly in response to the military stalemate after mid-1999. Such an evolution is typical of conflicts in general: combatants' motives usually change and may even shift back and forth—for example, from political to economic and back. Political and economic interests also often coexist, with one or the other becoming temporarily more important.[12]

As is demonstrated by the analyses of actors in this chapter, in the case of the Congo War, the main trend was for both domestic and foreign belligerents to enter the conflict as a result of political interests, including regime survival, fear of ethnic persecution, and a desire for influence over the DRC government. Economic interests became important for Congolese actors once they needed to generate funds to sustain their respective military campaigns. Economic interests became important to foreign actors when (a) they were faced with the need to sustain military operations—there were no quick victories; (b) they became cognizant of the profit-making opportunities available to them from their presence in the DRC; and (c) when entrepreneurs back home, seeking to capitalize on links to their militaries, persuaded them to exploit opportunities.

Note that *individuals* within DRC state institutions—indeed, within all belligerent and participant organizations—also developed personal economic agendas in addition to their institutional duties. This occurred for the most senior of officials, as evidenced by their involvement in companies explicitly created to exploit commercial opportunities in the DRC (see the following section for a description of some of these firms). Such behavior is in accordance with the DRC's history of state officials exploiting their authority and position for private gain.[13]

Economic agendas therefore emerged as a function of the war; war did not occur as a result of economic interests. To be sure, when economic interests did emerge, they did so with speed (within weeks rather than months) and became closely linked to, and at times have become indistinguishable from, political and military agendas.

The proclamations of Mai Mai leaders indicate that members of these militias were initially motivated by a desire to resist "foreigners"—a term they applied equally to Rwandans, Ugandans, *and* Banyamulenge and Banyarwanda. Such nomenclature is political in that it can be interpreted as nationalistic, but it is also ethnicist.[14] In the popular imagination, Mai Mai have been viewed by many Congolese and the DRC media as a resistance movement, but the reality is more complicated. Individual members have been motivated by a complex set of interests that often had more to do with unemployment, poverty, and social exclusion than with ethnicity or ideology. Furthermore, some Mai Mai militias coerced local people, including children, into joining their groups; some also looted villages and extorted taxes—behavior that is at odds with the idea that they are purely champions of a popular cause.[15]

The motives of the RCD factions and the MLC were also initially political but, and in contrast to the Mai Mai, these organizations hoped to gain control of the state or at least gain a seat at the table—partly as a result of ethnic concerns in the case of the RCD factions. The RCD's Banyamulenge and Banyarwanda members were concerned that the DRC government's increasing antagonism toward the RPA and reluctance to pursue the Interahamwe would evolve into a state-led campaign against them.

Irrespective of their original motives, all Congolese opposition groups soon faced the same challenge: the cost of waging war. To be sure, the RCD and MLC received some funding from the RPA and UPDF, and even the Mai Mai occasionally received air drops of food, equipment, and cash from the DRC government. But to seriously challenge their foes and to break the military stalemate, they were forced to undertake commercial activities that generated the income necessary to improve and expand their military capability. The economic activities of these groups eventually included extortion, looting, taxation of commerce, and the illicit production and trade of commodities.

Rebel involvement in the latter, especially the production and trade of colombo-tantalum (called coltan), became a notable feature of the Congo War. In the case of coltan, this can be traced to the spectacular rise in international prices for this mineral that occurred in late 2000. The metallic ore is a key element in the manufacture of cell phones, computer chips, and pagers. Market forces, in the form of exploding demand, caused coltan traders to focus intensely on the DRC—one of only a handful of countries producing the mineral[16]—and to seek links with the military forces that controlled the deposits. In turn, military forces made exploitation of coltan central to their own economic strategies. These relationships with commodities traders and private firms enabled belligerents to sustain their military operations. They presumably also enabled multinational companies that bought minerals from belligerents to supply their customers and maintain their share of the global market. There is evidence that of the four main processing firms—one each in China, the United States, Kazakhstan, and Germany—the latter two received supplies of coltan originating from the DRC, although the German firm has denied this.[17]

For the DRC government, economic interests have been inseparable from political interests: its sovereignty and survival were under assault, it had lost control of half of its territory along with the commerce within it that it previously taxed, and it had to fund a military campaign. The fiscal crisis precipitated by war and the loss of revenue was further exacerbated when one of the most important and historically dependable sources of funding for the state, foreign aid, reached its nadir in 1998.[18] Low levels of aid were probably the result of antipathy between the Laurent Kabila government (resentful at pressure to pay debts accumulated under Mobutu and increasingly bellicose in its diplomacy) and major donors (especially Belgium, the United States, the International Monetary Fund [IMF], and the World Bank).

To raise money, the DRC government adopted a two-pronged solution. First, it sought to extract more revenue by increasing taxation of its citizens. Due to the extreme inefficiency of the tax collection system, a legacy of the weak capacity of the Zairian state, there was a great incentive on the part of the government to exploit the remaining tax base more effectively.[19] In particular, it targeted activities that were relatively easy to control, such as imported consumer goods (e.g., bottled drinks, cigarettes, cooking oil, and gasoline). In 2000, fully 75 percent of state revenue came from taxes and customs duties, and only 3 percent came from Gécamines and Miba combined.[20] Second, it sought foreign commercial partners with the investment capital required for the exploitation of natural resources promising a quick return, such as diamonds. Prior to the war, the DRC government established contacts with many foreign companies to maintain and rehabilitate revenue-generating industries.[21] Some of these companies withdrew following the outbreak of hostilities as the war not only affected their ability to raise capital but also had a negative impact on their share price. Others, however, stayed and in some cases were persuaded by government officials to persist in organizing new ventures. In addition to such standard investments, the DRC government also offered foreign governments a direct exchange of public assets or a share in its parastatals in return for military support, such as weapons and troops. For example, diamond concessions in Kasai were allocated to senior Zimbabwean officials both as a reward for the Zimbabwean government's assistance to the Kabila government and as official repayment for cash advances and weapons and ammunitions previously provided by Harare.[22]

The preceding paragraph gives the impression of a somewhat disembodied bureaucracy rationally seeking to raise revenue to satisfy policy objectives. While there is some evidence of such a bureaucracy, these developments have been closely linked to the private appropriation of state resources and assets by all levels of the public service, as well as to predation by political and military elites. Joseph Kabila's sacking in January 2005 of six ministers and twelve parastatal chiefs following an investigation into corruption is evidence of the extent of private predation within state institutions.[23] But it is also evidence of institutional interests—in this case, Kabila ridding the bureaucracy of corrupt officials. It is probable that Kabila also satisfied some political interests by dismissing such high-profile figures.

At the start of the war, foreign governments were motivated by overwhelmingly political concerns. These are most easily explained in the case of Rwanda: it wanted a government in Kinshasa that was sympathetic to its interests, including regime survival (preventing cross-border attacks from the DRC) and the cessation of ethnic-based killings more generally. The Ugandan government was motivated by similarly strategic concerns. Despite tensions in the DRC-Uganda relationship, Museveni did not initiate military action against Laurent Kabila and was probably not aware of the Rwandan plan to airlift troops to Kitona.[24] However, Museveni and the UPDF feared that if the RPA and RCD were defeated, this would create uncertainty for the Ugandan government and instability on its border with the DRC. Concerned by this prospect and probably also influenced by close ties between the UPDF and the RPA, the Ugandan government allied itself with the anti-Kabila coalition.

Foreign allies of the DRC government were also initially motivated by political interests. In the case of Angola, the government had strategic concerns related to its conflict with UNITA.[25] Although the new AFDL government had cut off UNITA's vital supply networks through the DRC, in mid-1998, UNITA leader Jonas Savimbi visited Kigali, and UNITA vice president Antonio Dembo visited Kampala. This was interpreted as an ominous sign by the Angolan government, which was afraid that UNITA might secure new supplies from the Rwandan and Ugandan governments. In addition, the Rwandan government's attempt to topple Laurent Kabila by airlifting troops across the DRC to Bas-Congo in Angola's "backyard" had been planned and carried out without consulting or forewarning the Angolan government.[26] The Angolan government consequently sided with Laurent Kabila.

The lack of evidence regarding any substantial economic ties between Zimbabwe and the DRC (especially any government-to-government links) prior to the Congo War[27] suggests that commercial interests were also not at the forefront of Zimbabwean calculations. By contrast, there is evidence of political interests. President Mugabe had wanted to assert Zimbabwe's role within the SADC,[28] especially with a view to upstaging the South African government, which had established itself as a leading player in the organization despite having joined only four years earlier in 1994. In addition—and this is the Zimbabwean government's official explanation for intervention—the SADC charter included a collective security provision stating that in the event of a member being invaded, other members would come to its assistance.[29] The security provision made untenable suggestions that the DRC, a new member, should not receive support, as SADC would be viewed as a very ineffectual organization if it could not protect new members. Finally, the DRC government owed the Zimbabwean government U.S.$145 million for military equipment and other supplies.[30] Helping Laurent Kabila remain in power was a logical strategy for the Zimbabwean government if it hoped to recover outstanding debts. It is possible that these explanations are simply successful propagations of the Zimbabwean government, which was, in fact, prescient in its appreciation of economic opportunities in the DRC despite its lack of commercial relationships. Evidence for this, however, is lacking.

Regardless of foreign governments' initial political interests, the *cost* of their campaigns resulted in their explicitly seeking to offset military expenses. This was done in two main ways. First, the militaries from Uganda, Rwanda, and Zimbabwe organized commercial activities in the DRC. The Rwandan and Zimbabwean militaries specifically established commercial units for this purpose, although the Zimbabwean unit was only a cover for a private venture of four senior ruling-party officials.[31] Second, the Zimbabwean government encouraged Zimbabwean parastatals to create joint ventures with Congolese parastatals[32].

Commercial ventures that involved political and military elites or state institutional actors attracted private companies that sought to capitalize on their government's military presence in the DRC. This was especially the case for entrepreneurs who lacked contacts with civilian Congolese. Moreover, working with the military was safer than working without it and also reduced the transaction costs of establishing a presence in the DRC market.[33] Entrepreneurs from Rwanda and Zimbabwe were also motivated by poor domestic conditions.[34] From 1999 to 2000, entrepreneurs in these countries viewed the apparently easy entry into the DRC market on the back of government-negotiated access (in the Zimbabwean case) or militarily enforced access (in the Rwandan case) as strategies for economic survival.[35] War, once it started, contributed to this situation in the case of Zimbabwe. Economic conditions in Zimbabwe worsened following military intervention in the DRC precisely because of the Zimbabwean government's allocation of scarce domestic resources—such as fuel and foreign exchange—to its military campaign.[36] This was not the case for Rwanda, because the RPA's military campaign was largely self-funded by its commercial operations in the DRC and not from the state budget.

Independently of their military campaigns, regional economic expansion had been an element of the Zimbabwean and Ugandan governments' economic strategies since the early 1990s.[37] Both governments sought economic growth via exports of domestically manufactured products and increased investment in the region. Their involvement in the Congo War coincided with, and then facilitated, economic activities. In March 2000, the Zimbabwean government even organized a trade mission to Kinshasa of officials from the Ministry of Industry and Commerce, ZimTrade (a national association of exporters), various chambers of commerce, and individual entrepreneurs.

The Zimbabwean government also encouraged the private sector to invest in the DRC to avoid repeating the 'lesson' of its intervention in the Mozambican civil war. Despite their government's assistance to the Mozambican government in that conflict, Zimbabwean firms were given no privileged access to economic opportunities once a peace accord was signed. To avoid this in the DRC, the Zimbabwean government adopted an explicit policy of encouraging the private sector to exploit opportunities in the DRC, even while fighting was in progress.[38]

The conditions created by the war significantly contributed to the increased prevalence of economic interests. In war-torn states such as the DRC, where the leadership lacks the ability "to monopolize the means of exchange (e.g., vehicles, airports, roads, bank accounts, export authorizations, middlemen, importers) between a resource and the open economy" but has sought external assistance, an economic space is available for the leadership's "allies and subordinates to become autonomous through commercial or criminal activities based on local resources." [39] Precisely such a space opened up for Zimbabwean military and government officials, who became the chief allies of the DRC government, and for Rwandan and Ugandan forces in rebel zones. In a pattern observed elsewhere,[40] military forces were able to tax trade and create protection rackets due to their control over trading routes and major centers of commerce. These factors also contributed to the criminalization of the war economy—specifically, the entry into the economy by established criminal actors, such as illegal arms dealers, money launderers, and diamond smugglers. In addition, legitimate political and economic actors branched out into illegal activities; for example, Zimbabwean private firms and ZDF officials joined forces to smuggle diamonds.[41]

Insecurity caused by the conflict had varying effects on different companies. Some domestic and foreign commercial actors withdrew their capital or scaled down projects out of fear of the effect of conflict operations on their public share price or the security of their property rights and personnel. For example, Anglo-American restricted its operations to exploration and mothballed several proposed joint venture projects.[42] But insecurity also resulted in a tighter supply of goods—and consequently higher prices and larger profits—and other companies sought opportunities precisely because of the higher profits available. For example, many Zimbabwean entrepreneurs visited the DRC in late 1998 and early 1999, having heard there were excellent opportunities to buy minerals and to sell foodstuffs.[43]

The conditions created by the Congo War have not been the only factor responsible for these trends. The DRC state's generally weak capacity and incomplete control over its territory have attracted criminal actors and facilitated corruption among state officials. Unpaid salaries and poor government oversight also encouraged military actors, such as the FAZ and regional warlords, to develop their own commercial interests. Indeed, illegal activities and armed actors' involvement in business have been an entrenched element of trade and commerce in the DRC[44].

When war broke out, trade and commerce became concentrated in "border towns and internal trading gateways" and the trunk routes and airports that linked them[45]—a pattern that also occurred in Sierra Leone, Angola, Cambodia, and Afghanistan during their civil wars. These locations were the safest places to do business and subsequently became important sources of taxation revenue for the actors that controlled them. Taxation was especially important for RCD factions, the MLC, and the RPA and UPDF, as well as for individual members of these groups who used their positions to extract bribes. These organizations controlled the frontiers through which consumer goods were imported and timber, coffee, and minerals were exported. The UPDF and the RPA also controlled the air transport networks that were used to export gold, coltan, and diamonds out of antigovernment zones. Some of this "taxation" included extortion, but there was also legal trade where civilians were paid for their labor or goods. Progovernment forces also benefited from the concentration of trade and commerce into a small number of secure towns and roads. Mai Mai militias taxed goods passing through areas they controlled, and some Angolan units engaged in roadblock commerce, although this was not the Angolan government's policy. There are no reports of the ZDF generating funds by this method. The

DRC government, which legitimately extracted taxes from trade and commerce, also benefited from this pattern of concentration, as did government employees who took advantage of the situation to obtain bribes. In general, such behavior increased as the conflict progressed and formal salaries were increasingly left unpaid.

The conditions generated by the conflict have been responsible for one of the central features of the Congo War: the exploitation of primary commodities. Primary commodity production presents many advantages to actors in conflict situations. Unlike manufacturing, heavy industry, or even large-scale commercial agriculture, primary commodity production does not require complex information and transactions or a steady stream of specialized inputs. Primary commodity producers are therefore able to survive predatory taxation, unlike entrepreneurs in other sectors. Primary commodities offer non-state organizations, such as rebel forces, the additional advantage that they are "generic rather than branded products, and so their origin is much more difficult to determine."[46] These advantages were available to combatants in the Congo War. All rebel organizations and the Mai Mai, as well as the UPDF and RPA, sought to sell commodities they had illegally produced or acquired. Evidence of this is the rise in exports of gold and diamonds from Uganda and Rwanda during the war.[47] In contrast, the importance of primary commodity production for the DRC government was mixed, largely as a result of the varying "lootability" of the natural resources within the area it controlled: diamonds became highly significant, whereas *un*lootable copper, tin, and zinc lost much of their importance. Courtesy of their government's deals with the Kabila regime, Zimbabwean actors also became heavily involved in the production of diamonds and copper, although their interests in the latter diminished when they were unable to obtain sufficient investment capital to rehabilitate the sector or to generate continuous revenues.[48]

Primary commodity production was greatly facilitated by private companies, both foreign and domestic. Being in the business of natural resource exploitation, these companies needed to continue production and trade to remain profitable, notwithstanding the conflict. As minerals are site-specific, firms dependent on mineral exploitation are "condemned to developing resources where they can find them and where their investments have been made, whether that is in a war zone or not."[49] In addition, they will "maintain or even seek investment opportunities in war-torn areas, if those opportunities appear to warrant running the associated risks."[50] As the fixed location of minerals also makes mining companies vulnerable to extortion, there is ongoing negotiation between mining companies and combatants that centers on the companies' ability to produce revenue in return for protection. This was the case for the mining parastatals of the DRC government, as well as for the international firms that depended on minerals from the DRC. Rather than close down operations and leave once the war commenced, and potentially lose ground to competitors less averse to risk, many firms chose to continue their operations by dealing with whichever group controlled the area.

Actors and Their Economic Interests

The most significant economic activities to occur during the Congo War have been the result of ventures organized by three networks linking Congolese actors to the political, military, and business elites of Rwanda, Uganda, and Zimbabwe. The operations of these networks have been facilitated by their partnerships with foreign firms, although the latter also had discrete operations.

A major source of evidence for these interests comes from three reports produced by the UN: the *Report of the Panel of Experts on the Illegal Exploitation of Natural Resources and Other Forms of Wealth of the Democratic Republic of the Congo* (April 2001), the *Addendum to the Report* (November 2001), and the *Final Report* (October 2002).[51] While the findings of the reports have been generally accepted (although not by the belligerents concerned), their varying emphases have been criticized (see Chapter 4 for an analysis of the reports and their biases). The reports have made two major analytical contributions to analyses of the Congo War. First, they document the scope and nature of the commercial activities that sustained belligerents' military and political activities through the profits they generated (mostly from the exploitation of natural resources). Second, they detail the extensive networks and collaboration of military, political, and business elites that occurred during the course of the war. In fact, many prominent individuals pursued private interests while simultaneously performing their official organizational functions.

This section draws extensively on the three reports for evidence of economic interests and, unless otherwise cited, uses them as the relevant source of information (although direct quotes from the reports are cited). However, the section focuses only on the most analytically interesting commercial ventures. For detailed information regarding companies and their operations, readers should view the reports and the other documents cited in this section. See Table 3.1 for a list of major actors and their economic interests.

The DRC Government

The foundation for the DRC government's commercial links with actors in neighboring countries has been a combination of public and private companies controlled by a network of senior political officials. Most members of this group were not former "Mobutuists" but new elites: senior members of the AFDL or Congolese who returned to the DRC following the AFDL victory. The elite's growing economic control signaled the demise of the old patron-client relations that had dominated the economy since the 1970s.[52]

The economic activities of the government, and of individual government officials, have been largely carried out through commercial partnerships with foreign organizations. Laurent and Joseph Kabila used a private company—Comiex, a firm Laurent Kabila founded in the 1970s—to create joint ventures to exploit state assets for private gain. Most notably, Comiex formed Cosleg, a joint venture with the ZDF's commercial unit, Osleg, to mine diamonds. In February 2000, Kabila issued presidential decrees awarding a diamond concession to Cosleg

Table 3.1 Major Military Actors and Their Key Economic Interests in the DRC, 1998–2004

	Coffee	Gold	Coltan	Timber	Diamonds	Copper	Cobalt	Oil	Trade	The State
Progovernment forces										
DRC government				•	•	•	•	•		•
Zimbabwean government				•	•					•
Angolan government					•					•
Mai Mai	•	•			•				•	
Antigovernment forces										
Rwandan government	•	•	•	•					•	
Ugandan government	•	•	•	•	•				•	
RCD-Goma	•	•	•	•					•	
RCD-ML	•	•	•	•	•				•	
MLC	•	•	•		•				•	

Source: United Naations, *Report of the Panel of Experts on the Illegal Exploitation of Natural Resources and Other Forms of Wealth of the Democratic Republic of Congo* (New York: UN, April 2001).

and another to a Cosleg subsidiary, Sengamines.[53] The plan was to increase production by evicting artisanal miners, who had been granted rights under DRC law, and by adopting industrial methods.[54] This was a major blow to Miba, which had legal title to the concessions and was not consulted prior to their appropriation. It also did not receive compensation.

Despite its undermining of Miba's rights, the DRC government made other parastatals central to its efforts to generate revenue. Gécamines was permitted to form joint ventures with private companies to exploit cobalt, which was receiving historically high prices.[55] The government also created marketing parastatals through which all commodities had to be sold, starting with one for gold and diamonds in January 1999.[56] In the case of diamonds, the marketing parastatal was replaced, in August 2000, with an exclusive buying monopoly operated by International Diamond Industries (IDI) of Israel.[57] Both mechanisms failed to generate additional revenue. *Comptoirs* (diamond traders) were unhappy with the former due to the high cost of license fees and unhappy with the latter due to the low prices offered by IDI.[58] The result was that they smuggled their stones to neighboring countries rather than sell through the new mechanisms, causing a *reduction* in government revenue as official production and exports plunged. It is possible that these marketing mechanisms were created by government officials to maximize their personal opportunities for private predation. However, given that at this time the DRC government had few sources of income (including from foreign aid), the effort that went into creating these mechanisms suggests that they really were the result of an institutional initiative rather than officials' pernicious attempt to create further opportunities for predation.

In a departure from policies dating from the 1960s, the government also pursued an agenda of economic liberalization of the mining industry. In July 2002, parliament passed a new mining code—developed with assistance from the World Bank—that promoted "mineral development by the private sector with the principal role of the state to promote and regulate the development of the mining industry by the private sector."[59] This was a radical development in a previously state-run industry.

Finally, the government allowed state institutions to develop ties to firms operating in the rebel zone in order to exploit commercial opportunities there. For example, in mid-2001, the government invited the Belgian diamond company Arslanian Frères, which openly operated in Kisangani, to invest in a multimillion-dollar project aimed at reorganizing Miba.

The RCD-Goma

The illicit exploitation of coltan and diamonds has been an important source of revenue for the RCD-Goma. In early 2000, Adolphe Onusumba, leader of RCD-Goma, declared, "We raise more or less $200,000 per month from diamonds . . . Coltan gives us more: a million dollars a month."[60] While this figure may have been an exaggeration, the evidence suggest that coltan-related activities were highly profitable, although it remains unclear what proportion of these revenues remained with the rebel group and what proportion was passed on to the RPA.[61] Despite the RPA eventually obtaining a near monopoly on some economic activities within eastern DRC, the RCD-Goma managed to continue operating a largely independent network of companies that bought and sold coltan, as well as other businesses through which it was able to raise funds.[62] Many senior RCD-Goma officials also set up businesses in partnership with Rwandan colleagues. These private joint ventures became junior players in the economy of the RCD Rwandan zone, although the RPA's commercial operations have remained economically dominant. As occurred within all rebel groups, senior individuals have been the largest beneficiaries of the RCD-Goma's commercial activities. Certainly, few of the taxes collected have been used to provide public goods for the local population.

The RCD-ML

Like the RCD-Goma, the RCD-ML pursued its economic interests and developed economic strategies in close collaboration with its foreign backer, the UPDF. But the UPDF held a looser rein than the RPA over its Congolese allies. The RCD-ML's major economic activities involved some coltan production and taxing of trade. Entrepreneurs importing goods from Uganda into the DRC—a trade that involved thousands of containers of consumer goods—were required to pay a fee averaging $8,000 per container to the RCD-ML. A portion of the revenues were diverted to UPDF officers and the RCD-ML reportedly used none of the revenue for public services.

These activities were facilitated by the RCD-ML's control of Bunia, a large and important trading center 20 miles from the Ugandan border, located on a major trade route stretching from eastern DRC, through Uganda, to Kenya and the Gulf states. Bunia's importance as a source of revenue is probably the reason the RCD-ML forces retreated to Bunia following clashes between UPDF and RPA troops in 2000. The loss of the town to RPA forces would have been a financial disaster for both the organization and its Ugandan allies.

The MLC

The president of the MLC is Jean-Pierre Bemba, son of a powerful Mobutu-era politician who owned a trade and transport conglomerate operating throughout northern DRC and who was at one stage part of the Laurent Kabila government (father and son became estranged during the conflict). Other senior MLC figures also owned businesses in northern DRC, interests that had been targeted by the Laurent Kabila government, including confiscation of property, imposition of taxes, and general harassment. Herein lay the origins of the MLC's opposition to that government. An exception to such entrepreneur-rebels is the MLC's secretary-general, Olivier Kamitatu. While also from a wealthy family, Kamitatu had few economic interests in the northern DRC to protect, suggesting he was more motivated by political concerns.[63]

The MLC's major source of funding was the taxes it extracted from private businesses. The Victoria Group, headquartered in Kampala and working closely with senior Ugandan military officials, was an important single source. It had gold, diamond, and coffee trading operations throughout northern DRC, although diamond production was largely confined to the northeast Ituri region, which was under the control of the UPDF. The MLC also taxed local businesses that imported consumer goods and exported coffee and timber—the two most significant primary commodities within MLC territory (there are no large mining interests in northern DRC).

The high taxes imposed by the MLC, in some cases double-digit, caused resentment among local businesspeople. In fact, it was Bemba's imposition of high taxes on the diamond industry in Ituri during his appointment as leader of the short-lived FLC that contributed to the breakdown of the coalition.[64]

Mai Mai Militias

Compared to rebel organizations, much less detail is known about the economic activities of Mai Mai militias. It is not clear what interests figured in the calculations of Mai Mai members at the outset of the conflict, but militias would very quickly have had to organize commercial activities or loot in order to sustain military campaigns. The degree to which individual militia members, especially leaders, gained private advantage from such activities is also not clear.

Eyewitness accounts documented by nongovernmental organizations (NGOs) early in the war report that both collectively and as individuals some Mai Mai militias routinely extorted food, supplies, and money from civilians and waged military campaigns over control of mineral deposits and roads on which they could erect roadblocks.[65] Some militias developed links with Interahamwe and Burundian anti-Tutsi Forces de Défense de la Démocratie (FDD) based in the DRC in order to produce and trade gold and to smuggle contraband. Others were used by chiefs to enforce their decisions regarding the distribution of customary lands and by autochtonous businesspeople in North Kivu to intimidate Tutsi rivals.[66] The links to autochtonous businesspeople are in keeping with the perception that Mai Mai are primarily focused on resisting "foreigners" (racism notwithstanding), but such collaborations also suggest a mercenary element, for presumably the Mai Mai received something in return for their services. These kinds of relationships probably also laid the foundation for the extensive commercial networks that have developed over the course of the war and for which the coercive power of the Mai Mai militias has become a critical component.

Congolese Entrepreneurs

Private Congolese entrepreneurs played a pivotal role in the war economy in all zones and were essential to the functioning of the three main commercial networks. Some entrepreneurs were significant commercial actors prior to the war, but others were specifically selected by their military patrons to facilitate their activities and replaced those who dominated trade prior to the conflict. Expatriate entrepreneurs, typically carrying Greek, Belgian, Indian, Lebanese, or Pakistani passports, were established players in the natural resources sector and in retail and wholesale commerce.[67] Lebanese traders were especially prominent in the diamond industry. One notable private firm was the Enterprise Générale Malta Forrest (EGMF) company, headed by its DRC-born, Belgian expatriate chairman, Georges Forrest. Forrest had several profitable joint ventures to exploit cobalt and copper involving Gécamines, foreign mineral processing firms, and Belgian banks. Expatriate entrepreneurs also worked opportunistically to broker import and export deals. Despite occasional surges of xenophobia that curtailed their commercial activities, expatriates adapted to the conflict by shifting their activities into black market trades for diamonds, gold, and currency—sectors in which they had advantages over some Congolese due their national and international (ethnic-based) trade networks, as well as foreign bank accounts that enabled financial transactions to occur in a foreign currency and beyond the reach of DRC officials.

Zimbabwe

At the center of trade between Zimbabwe and the DRC has been a commercial network rooted in senior government and military officials from the ruling political party, the Zimbabwe African National Union–Patriotic Front (ZANU-PF). The most politically and economically significant ventures of this network involved copper, cobalt, and diamonds. Senior government and party officials developed partnerships with a group of wealthy private entrepreneurs, as well as with members of their extended families who were not civil servants but who were probably also ZANU-PF members. They also had overlapping public and private interests in what were ostensibly state-sponsored projects.[68]

Despite the extensive media coverage given to Zimbabwean commercial involvement in the DRC, most ventures have yielded few profits and experienced many difficulties. First, Zimbabwean investors were hampered by the inefficient DRC banking sector, which made simple payments difficult. Second, many Congolese did not pay their debts to Zimbabwean firms—the DRC state itself owed money to two Zimbabwean parastatals. Third, a weak and corrupt legal system made it almost impossible for Zimbabweans to ensure that their contracts with Congolese were enforced. How can the difficulties and lack of profitability faced by Zimbabwean business ventures be reconciled with Zimbabwean interest in the DRC? To make profits, entrepreneurs had to operate in sectors where they were not subject to competition and where it was easy to produce whatever commodity was involved.[69] It is therefore not surprising that the most enduring commercial involvement involving Zimbabweans has been in the diamond sector, because this is one of the few industries to offer quick profits. And the speed of profits was surely important to Zimbabweans if their ability to exploit diamonds was contingent on the continuation of the war and their military importance to the DRC government.[70]

Angola

Economic involvement by Angolan individuals and organizations has been of a much smaller scope and scale than that of Rwandans, Ugandans, or Zimbabweans. The only documented venture, between the National Angolan Fuel Company (Sonangol) and Comiex, was to distribute and retail Angolan petroleum products in the DRC and to jointly explore for oil off the DRC-Angola coast. The joint venture, Sonangol-Congo, had the appearance of a bilateral government project rather than a project organized by a network of elites for their private interest, but

Sonangol was controlled by Jose Dos Santos, the Angolan president, and Comiex was controlled by Joseph Kabila.[71] The Angolan government also reportedly demanded compensation in the form of diamond concessions for military expenses it incurred assisting the DRC government.[72]

Rwanda

The network that organized much of the economic activity between rebel zones and Rwanda was directly controlled by the Rwandan government. The key organization was the "Congo Desk," a unit of the Department of External Relations in the Rwandan Ministry of Defence. The UN Expert Panel has alleged that the Congo Desk was the link between the commercial and military activities of the RPA and described it as the RPA's "commercial wing."[73] Officials of the RPA organized many ventures, including establishing diamond- and coltan-buying *comptoirs* in Kisangani and Bukavu, respectively, as well as coltan mining and the contracting of aircraft to transport coltan ore. These activities were organized on behalf of the Rwandan government not for their private interests, although side payments to the individuals involved were probably an element in many of these deals. Individuals with close links to international criminal networks also worked closely with the network centered on the Congo Desk, especially in providing aircraft to transport minerals, military personnel, and armaments to and from zones controlled by the RCD-Goma and RPA.[74] Another element of this network involved Rwandan companies with links to members of Rwanda's governing elite, which brokered deals with international minerals trading firms.[75] The RPA cultivated Congolese contacts to assist its commercial operations, but it also sought to minimize its dependence on them. For example, the RPA took direct control of several coltan operations by stationing troops at mine sites; it then flew the ore to Kigali, bypassing Congolese intermediaries and reducing costs in the process.[76] The Rwandan-based network was all-encompassing, involving international, regional, and local actors. It controlled production, transport, and wholesale sales of minerals extracted from eastern DRC.

The RPA's economic activity also extended to theft, including the seizure of commodity stocks and the looting of household property from communities suspected of supporting progovernment militias.[77] The UN Panel of Experts has alleged that the RPA raised funds by extorting protection money from businesses, from a 5 percent tax on diamond and coltan *comptoirs*, from profits it received as a shareholder in several companies, and from contributions from RCD-Goma—many of these revenues coming from the licensing fees RCD-Goma demanded from *comptoirs*. Until mid-2000, these fees, which were an estimated $200,000 per month, were evenly shared by the RCD-Goma and the RPA. However, as the conflict wore on, the RPA demanded a greater share.

Unlike most Zimbabwean activities, Rwandan ventures were highly profitable. One report has estimated that coltan exports earned the Rwandan government approximately $40 million in net profits during the eighteen months from mid-1999 to the end of 2000.[78] The UN panel estimated that in 1999 alone, the combined activities of the Congo Desk—including all taxes, sales profits, and other contributions—realized about $320 million.

Uganda

The network between Uganda and the territory controlled by the UPDF and its allies in the DRC has featured a coterie of senior military officials close to President Museveni and has been more decentralized and less hierarchical than the Rwandan network. Most of these officials formed private companies to conduct their commercial activities and then worked with a Congolese affiliate. They have not engaged in trade in the name of the UPDF, and in this respect they are different from the individuals behind the commercial units of the ZDF and FAC. Lebanese expatriates figured prominently in this network, brokering the transport and sale of many of the commodities produced and traded through the network, as well as having positions in some of the companies formed by military officials. The Ugandan network has some similarities with the Rwandan network in that it involved individuals with criminal records. It also relied on a set of Congolese intermediaries, many of whom were members of, or linked to, the UPDF's political ally in the DRC—the RCD-ML.

Organizations, companies, and individuals involved in the Uganda-based network have been involved in a wide range of endeavors, including exporting a wide range of primary commodities *from* the DRC and shipping weapons and consumer goods *to* the DRC for sale in UPDF and MLC territory. While much of this trade involved payment for goods, some members of the network also engaged in theft.

Like the Rwandan network, the Ugandan network also generated profits. Uganda has always been a conduit for a small amount of diamond exports, but the value of exports increased sevenfold from 1997 to

1998. Diamond exports peaked at $1.8 million in 1999, dropping to $1.3 million in 2000. The volume of other minerals also increased: gold exports in 1999 and 2000 were approximately double those of 1997; coltan exports in 2000 were *twenty-seven* times larger than those of 1997; and cobalt exports in 2000 were four times greater than those of 1999. However, *which* individuals, companies, and organizations gained from these exports remains unclear, including the proportion of profits, if any, that accrued to the Ugandan government.

Foreign Companies

The reports of the UN Panel of Experts have listed individuals and companies from twenty-six countries in Africa, Asia, Europe, and North America, with operations that have involved the exploitation of natural resources. These commercial actors come from across the economic spectrum, including Western multinationals, specialized commodities firms, foreign banks, and both midsized firms and small-scale traders— the latter especially from southern and eastern Africa. Trade in consumer goods and foodstuffs occupied the smaller private traders, but the most politically and economically significant ventures were in the minerals subsector and involved large companies. Some of these companies had ventures in the DRC prior to the war and were reluctant to abandon their ventures. As discussed, natural resources firms were especially constrained because they could not relocate their assets or ore deposits. Other companies were recent arrivals, having been attracted by the government's new liberalization policies for the minerals sector.

The operations of many larger firms with mining operations or projects in the preparatory stage in the government zone were made possible by financing from foreign banks, although, with the onset of war, it became very difficult to obtain investment capital or insurance for new projects. Nevertheless, banks have been able to maintain profitable operations despite the war and economic stagnation by demanding high transaction fees for deals in the mining sector.

Foreign companies with interests in the antigovernment zone overwhelmingly worked through local partners or companies linked to individuals in the RPA and UPDF, rather than establishing direct operations. Like firms operating in the government zone, these companies also focused on minerals, especially coltan which was mostly found in antigovernment zones. Especially important to the war economy of these zones were firms that bought or processed coltan or diamonds.

Conclusion

The Congo War has been a multilevel conflict involving a diverse range of belligerents and participants. It has featured extensive violence against civilians and competition for control of natural resources and trading routes and has profoundly undermined already weak state institutions, as well as law and order more generally. The cost imperative of waging war and the presence of conditions that created many opportunities for profit making resulted in actors developing economic interests in addition to their original political and security interests. For some actors, economic interests eventually superseded initial motives; for others, economic interests have became an equal part of a larger combination of interests. The economic interests that have emerged mostly did so as a consequence of the conflict, and not vice versa.

The resulting war economy has been dominated by armed actors working in close collaboration with domestic and foreign private companies, as well as criminal actors—indeed, illegal activities have been an intrinsic element of the war economy. Together, these actors organized comprehensive commercial networks that relied upon violent and predatory strategies to exploit natural resources, fix prices, and extort the civilian population. The uncertainty caused by these predatory tactics, coupled with the breakdown of the rule of law and with the fighting in general, has led these networks to focus on activities that require few investments and yield quick profits—that is, extracting taxes from trade and exploiting certain natural resources.

Wars like this are difficult to resolve. Compared to conflicts without great spoils, the conditions they create result in highly lucrative opportunities that give stakeholders more and greater incentives to maintain those conditions rather than to seek peace. Belligerents may consequently choose to "spoil" the peace by remaining armed, resisting demobilization, and continuing to use violence. This is because violence allows some belligerents to achieve their political goals and ensures their economic survival; for other belligerents, violence brings both political gains and, more than just survival, economic *richesses*. Postconflict environments can also be unattractive to foreign belligerents because any peace deal usually requires their repatriation, preventing their continued exploitation of economic opportunities. In the case of the Congo War, the postconflict alternatives to wartime activities are meager. The economic opportunities that do exist will probably narrow in the future as a result of the DRC government's liberalization policies that have attracted capital-rich, technically advanced foreign companies that can easily out-compete domestic networks in the production of primary commodities.

This raises the question as to why combatants decided to negotiate a peace accord. The short answer is that the peace accord does not threaten their economic interests because it does not substantively address economic issues. Furthermore, a political settlement creates additional economic opportunities for rebel leaders because it gives them access to state positions and resources that allow them to pursue their private interests (Chapter 4 explores these issues in detail). But a political settlement has also been a valuable end in itself for Congolese participants in the peace accords and their foreign backers. That is, economic interests have not necessarily been more important than other interests. For example, a hypothetical peace accord that resolved economic grievances but not political or security interests—for example, no agreement by the DRC government to target anti-Tutsi militias—would not have been acceptable to the RCD-ML or RCD-Goma (and certainly not to Rwanda).

The peace accords developed for the DRC have similarities to those negotiated in another country involving multiple causes: Burma. A quick comparison of the two cases illuminates the advantages the Lusaka accords brought the Kabila government and participating rebel factions. In both the DRC and Burma, central authorities negotiated peace accords (several in the Burma case) that allowed them and selected rebel parties to continue exploiting natural resources.[79] Such agreements not only allowed central authorities and rebels to reduce war expenditure, but also opened up new commercial opportunities for government and rebel parties. In the case of Burma, another advantage for the governing State Law and Order Restoration Committee (SLORC) was that peace accords allowed it to increase its control over peripheral regions and cross-border trade. This advantage is yet to occur for the pro-Kabila elements of the DRC's transitional government because the MLC and RCD factions continue to exercise military control over their regions and border areas (notwithstanding the creation of the new unified national army, the Forces Armées de la République Démocratique du Congo). In both countries, peace accords have increased central authorities' control over international relations, especially between foreign governments and domestic groups. A key difference is that in Burma, peace accords do not provide for power-sharing arrangements between the SLORC and rebel ethnic minority groups,[80] whereas in the

DRC, rebel parties have been brought into the transitional government. Another difference is that ethnicity has no official profile in the negotiations in the DRC, although it utterly pervades all popular discourse on the conflict. In this respect, ethnicity is a bit like the "hidden script" that Grignon argues guides negotiations over economic interests (see Chapter 4).

To a large degree, the challenges that remain in the DRC do so because of the nature of the peace agreement that is now in place. An immediate challenge is to restore property and livelihoods to civilians affected by the conflict. Another is to disentangle the extensive criminal and illegal elements from legitimate economic activity, especially the illegal exploitation of natural resources, but also to end corruption and extortion. The United Nations Panel of Experts' *Final Report* on the illegal exploitation of natural resources in the DRC identifies the individuals and organizations allegedly involved in such activities,[81] but this list inadvertently illuminated another challenge: many of the commercial actors named will necessarily be players in the *legal* production of primary commodities because of their role as investors, producers, and processors in the global minerals market. The DRC government is probably unlikely to want, or even be able, to sanction commercial actors involved in the illegal exploitation of natural resources during the war. However, the reconstruction effort must at least focus on creating conditions that encourage legitimate investment in the future. In addition to macroeconomic and fiscal reform, this requires secure property rights and judicial reform—that is, capable state institutions.

But, one reason for the weakness of state institutions has been their lack of legitimacy, and overcoming this requires more than just institutional strengthening. Political leaders and state officials must be made accountable to the public or develop a nationalist vision that, at least occasionally, places the collective good before their own private interests. Some scholars, including Emizet Kisangani in Chapter 5, argue that customary authorities have the legitimacy necessary to make DRC politics more transparent and more responsive to the populace. But this may not be the case. Labeled the "prostitutes" of Mobutu during his regime,[82] many chiefs have now developed such a diverse set of private interests involving belligerents and participants that one must be skeptical of their motives. Unfortunately, the DRC government is also virtually bereft of "clean" politicians, a situation that has not been improved by the entry into government of rebel organizations with the kinds of interests outlined in this chapter.

Notes

1. Jeremy M. Weinstein, "Africa's 'Scramble for Africa': Lessons of a Continental War," *World Policy Journal* (summer 2000): 11–20.

2. Paul Collier, "Doing Well Out of War: An Economic Perspective," in Mats Berdal and David M. Malone, eds., *Greed and Grievance: Economic Agendas in Civil Wars* (Boulder, Colo.: Lynne Rienner, 2000).

3. Author interview with former Medécins sans Frontières (MSF)–Belgium worker formerly stationed in the Kivu area, December 2001.

4. Michael Nest, "The Evolution of a Fragmented State: The Case of the Democratic Republic of Congo" (Ph.D. diss., New York University, May 2002), especially Chapters 4 and 5.

5. Zimbabwean entrepreneurs' interest in pursuing opportunities in the DRC, for example, corresponded with the ebb and flow of the war. There were rebel advances in northern Katanga from September to November 1998, and again from April to May 1999 (author's confidential interview with a humanitarian aid worker formerly stationed in Lubumbashi, January 2002). Most private (nonstate) Zimbabwean entrepreneurs visited the DRC after the first advance. Their disenchantment with the DRC arose after the second advance. The two may not be directly related, but media reports that the Copperbelt would be invaded would surely have dissuaded many Zimbabwean entrepreneurs from investing in such a market. In November 2000, rebel forces made another (failed) advance into southeast Katanga, and by this time it appears that most Zimbabweans still involved in the DRC were involved in government-to-government ventures or were doing business with either the FAC or the ZDF (Nest, "The Evolution of a Fragmented State," p. 288).

6. Philippe Le Billon, "The Political Ecology of War: Natural Resources and Armed Conflicts," *Political Geography* 20 (2001): 571.

7. Human Rights Watch reported that Angolan and FAC troops engaged in looting on several occasions. See *Casualties of War: Civilians, Rule of Law, and Democratic Freedoms* (New York: HRW, 1999), p. 15. There is little evidence that ZDF personnel engaged in such behavior.

8. United Nations, *Report of the Panel of Experts on the Illegal Exploitation of Natural Resources and Other Forms of Wealth of the Democratic Republic of Congo* (New York: UN, 2001).

9. Author interview with former MSF worker; Joanne Cosete, *The War Within the War: Sexual Violence Against Women and Girls in Eastern Congo* (New York: Human Rights Watch, 2002).

10. See the three reports of the United Nations *Panel of Experts on the Illegal Exploitation of Natural Resources and Other Forms of Wealth of the Democratic Republic of Congo.*

11. Not all primary commodities are amenable to conflict production. Copper, tin, and zinc—all important to the DRC government due to their long-term potential—were not amenable to conflict production because they have high weight-to-value ratios, requiring large-scale, capital-intensive, industrial production and a disciplined and skilled labor force. In contrast, colombo-tantalum, gold, and especially diamonds have low weight-to-value ratios. (In com-

parison to copper, cobalt could also be considered to have a low weight-to-value, but because it is produced in conjunction with copper ore, it is not amenable to conflict production.) Depending on the geological features of coltan, gold, and diamond deposits, these minerals may be cheaply produced, using artisanal methods, and easily exported. Michael L. Ross describes these differences in terms of "lootable" versus "unlootable" commodities. See Michael L. Ross, "Oil, Drugs, and Diamonds: The Varying Roles of Natural Resources in Civil War," in Karen Ballentine and Jake Sherman, eds., *The Political Economy of Armed Conflict: Beyond Greed and Grievance* (Boulder, Colo.: Lynne Rienner, 2003), pp. 47–70.

   12. Ballentine and Sherman, *The Political Economy of Armed Conflict.*

   13. See John F. Clark, "Zaire: The Bankruptcy of the Extraction State," in Leonardo A. Villalón and Philip A. Huxtable, eds., *The African State at a Critical Juncture: Between Disintegration and Reconfiguration* (Boulder, Colo.: Lynne Rienner, 1998), pp. 109–125; William Reno, "Sovereignty and Personal Rule in Zaire," *African Studies Quarterly* 1, no. 3 (1997), available at www.clas.ufl.edu/africa/asq/v1/3/4.html; Crawford Young and Thomas Turner, *The Rise and Decline of the Zairian State* (Madison: University of Wisconsin Press, 1985); Thomas Callaghy, *The State-Society Struggle: Zaire in Comparative Perspective* (New York: Columbia University Press, 1984); Michael G. Schatzberg, *Politics and Class in Zaire: Bureaucracy, Business, and Beer in Lisala* (New York: Africana Publishing, 1980).

   14. The first use of the term *Mai Mai* can be traced to militias who specifically sought to counter Banyarwanda encroachment into autochthonous tribal lands in the Fizi-Baraka region of South Kivu in 1960. See Frank Van Acker and Koen Vlassenroot, "Les "Maï-Maï" et les functions de la violence milicienne dans l'est du Congo," *Politique Africaine,* no. 84 (December 2001): 108.

   15. See Human Rights Watch, *Reluctant Recruits: Children and Adults Forcibly Recruited for Military Service in North Kivu* (New York: HRW, 2001); HRW, *Casualties of War*; Frank Van Acker and Koen Vlassenroot, "Youth and Conflict in Kivu: Komona Clair," *Journal of Humanitarian Affairs* (2000), available at http://222.jha.ac/greatlakes/b004.htm.

   16. Larry D. Cunningham, "Columbium (Niobium) and Tantalum," in the U.S. Geological Survey's *Minerals Yearbook* (Washington, D.C.: U.S. Bureau of Mines, 2003).

   17. Jeroen Cuvelier and Tim Raeymaekers, *Supporting the War Economy in the DRC: European Companies and the Coltan Trade; Five Case Studies* (Brussels: International Peace Information Service, 2002).

   18. Organization for Economic Cooperation and Development, *Geographical Distribution of Financial Flows to Aid Recipients* (Paris: Development Assistance Committee, various years).

   19. Author interview with Dikanga Kazadi, political adviser to the governor of Katanga, Lubumbashi, November 1999.

   20. Banque Centrale du Congo, Ministry of Finance, as reported in the Economist Intelligence Unit's *DRC Country Report,* May 2001, p. 44.

   21. Hugues LeClercq, "Le jeu des intérêts miniers dans le conflit congolais," paper prepared for the seminar "The Internal and Regional Dynamics of the Congo Crisis in 1999," January 5–6, 1999 (Brussels: Conflict Prevention

Network); François Misser, "Fools Rush In . . . and Out?" *African Business*, March 1998, pp. 27–28; "Mining for Trouble," *Africa Confidential* 37, no. 25, December 1996, pp. 5–6.

22. Eric Kennes, "Le secteur minier au Congo: 'Déconnexion' et descente aux enfers," in Filip Reyntjens and Stefaan Marysse, eds., *L'Afrique des Grands Lacs, Annuaire 1999–2000* (Antwerp: Centre d'Etude de la Région des Grands Lacs d'Afrique, 2000), pp. 299–343.

23. South African Broadcasting Corporation, "Congo Replaces 11 Ministers in Government Shuffle," January 4, 2005, available at www.sabc.gov.za.

24. Evidence for this is the timing of Ugandan troops' entry into the DRC in late August, *after* ZDF and Angolan troops had intervened on Laurent Kabila's behalf. See John F. Clark, "Explaining Ugandan Intervention in Congo: Evidence and Interpretations," *Journal of Modern African Studies* 39, no. 2 (2001): 261–287.

25. UNITA was probably also a factor in the Namibian government's involvement. Namibia suffered cross-border attacks by UNITA after 2000 when it permitted Angolan troops to pursue UNITA forces that had retreated into Namibian territory. The Namibian government may therefore have allied itself with the AFDL government for similar reasons as the Angolan government. In addition, the president of Namibia, Sam Nujoma, who was also a close ally of Robert Mugabe from the days of liberation struggle in the 1970s and 1980s, may have shared similar perceptions regarding the South African government's aspirations for regional political hegemony.

26. Thomas Turner, "Angola's Role in the Congo War," in Clark, *The African Stakes of the Congo War*, pp. 75–92.

27. Nest, "The Evolution of a Fragmented State," pp. 275–276.

28. United Nations, *Addendum to the Report of the Panel of Experts on the Illegal Exploitation of Natural Resources and Other Forms of Wealth of the Democratic Republic of Congo* (New York: United Nations, 2001), p. 16.

29. Article 4 of the Declaration and Treaty of the SADC Charter (1992).

30. Economist Intelligence Unit, *DRC Country Report* (London: EIU, 1998).

31. "ZDF Chief in DRC Mining Ventures," *The Standard* (Harare), September 26–October 2, 1999, p. 1. Notably, the company was formally registered on December 7, 1998, four months after the ZDF entered into the Congo War (registration documents sighted by the author at the Zimbabwean Registrar of Companies, Harare). This suggests that it was created to exploit opportunities newly available to the company's owners *following* their involvement in the Congo War, rather than being the result of a prewar commercial strategy to exploit the DRC.

32. Author interview with Mike Chivhanganye, former Zimbabwean trade attaché to the DRC, Harare, March 6, 2000.

33. Author interview with Washington C. Mhlanga, divisional manager (metals), Minerals Marketing Corporation of Zimbabwe, Harare, December 1999; David Shearer, "Africa's Great War," *Survival* 41, no. 2 (summer 1999): 98.

34. For Rwanda, see Koen Vlassenroot and Hans Romkema, "The

Emergence of a New Order? Resources and War in Eastern Congo," *Journal of Humanitarian Assistance,* available online at www.jha.ac/articles/a111.htm, p. 4. For Zimbabwe, see Michael Nest, "Ambitions, Profits and Loss: Zimbabwean Economic Involvement in the Democratic Republic of the Congo," *African Affairs* 400, no. 100 (July 2001): 469–490; Paul Raftopoulos, "Briefing: Zimbabwe's 2002 Presidential Election," *African Affairs* 101, no. 404 (2002): 413–426.

35. Author interview with John Mangudya, assistant chief executive, Zimtrade, Harare, March 2000; confidential interview with a Zimbabwean entrepreneur with retail interests in the DRC, Harare, March 2000.

36. Economist Intelligence Unit, *Zimbabwe Country Report* (London: EIU, 2000).

37. For Zimbabwe, see Nest, "Ambitions, Profits and Loss"; David Compagnon, "'Mugabe and Partners (PVT) LTD' ou l'investissement politique du champ économique," *Politique Africaine* 81 (March 2001): 101–119. For Uganda, see John F. Clark, "Explaining Ugandan Intervention in Congo: Evidence and Interpretations," *Journal of Modern African Studies* 39, no. 2: 261–287. Clark disagrees that the Ugandan government's embracing of liberal economic policies alone accounts for Ugandan intervention.

38. Author interview with Chivhanganye, Harare, March 6, 2000.

39. Le Billon, "The Political Ecology of War," p. 571.

40. See William Stanley, *The Protection Racket State: Elite Politics, Military Extortion, and Civil War in El Salvador* (Philadelphia: Temple University Press, 1996); Darini Rajasingham, "The Dangers of Devolution: The Hidden Economies of Armed Conflict," in Robert Rotberg, ed., *Creating Peace in Sri Lanka* (Washington, D.C.: Brookings Institution Press, 1999); Adekeye Adebajo, *Building Peace in West Africa: Liberia, Sierra Leone, and Guinea-Bissau* (Boulder, Colo.: Lynne Rienner, 2002).

41. Author's confidential interview with Zimbabwean entrepreneur collaborating with the ZDF to illegally export diamonds from the DRC, Harare, December 1999.

42. Author interview with Anglo-American executive, Johannesburg; June 1998.

43. Author interviews with Zimbabwean entrepreneurs.

44. For example, regional strongmen or "warlords" that flourished under Mobutu were all involved in illegal commerce. See Reno, "Sovereignty and Personal Rule in Zaire."

45. Le Billon, "The Political Ecology of War," p. 571.

46. Paul Collier, "Doing Well Out of War, p. 94.

47. United Nations, *Report of the Panel of Experts.*

48. See Nest, "The Evolution of a Fragmented State," Chapter 7.

49. International Committee of the Red Cross, *War, Money, and Survival* (Geneva: ICRC, 2002), p. 45.

50. Ibid.

51. All three reports were published by the United Nations, New York.

52. Erik Kennes, "Footnotes to the Mining Story," *Review of African Political Economy,* no. 93/94 (2002): 604.

53. "Glittering Prizes from the War," *Africa Confidential* 41, no. 11, May 26, 2000, p. 2.

54. Réseau Européen Congo, *Bulletin No. 7* (July 2001).

55. Jef Maton, "Congo 1997–1999: La guerre des minerais et la fin temporaire des espoirs" (manuscript, University of Ghent, May 1999).

56. Economist Intelligence Unit, *DRC Country Report* (London: EIU, February 1999).

57. Ellen Kickmeyer, "Congo Cancels Israeli-Diamond Supply," Associated Press, April 21, 2001.

58. Economics Intelligence Unit, *DRC Country Report* (London: EIU, 1998), p. 36.

59. George J. Coakley, *The Mineral Industry of Congo (Kinshasa)*, U.S. Geological Survey (Washington, D.C.: U.S. Bureau of Mines, 2002), p. 10.2.

60. Karl Vick, "In the Waging of Congo's Wars, Vital Ore Plays Crucial Role," *International Herald Tribune*, March 20, 2001.

61. See Jeroen Cuvelier and Tim Raeymaekers, *European Companies and the Coltan Trade: An Update*, Part 2 (Brussels: International Peace Information Service, 2002); Aloys Tegera, Sofia Mikolo, and Dominic Johnson, *The Coltan Phenomenon: How a Rare Mineral Has Changed the Life of the Population of War-Torn North Kivu Province in the East of the DRC* (Goma, DRC: Pole Institute, 2002).

62. Correspondence with Elisabeth Sancery, political affairs officer, UN Organizing Mission in the Democratic Republic of Congo (MONUC), 1999–2002.

63. Tatiana Carayannis, "Rebels with a Cause? A Study of the Mouvement de Libération du Congo," paper delivered at the African Studies Association annual conference, Washington, D.C., December 5–8, 2002.

64. Tatiana Carayannis, "Hybrid Wars, Conflict Networks, and Multilateral Responses: The Congo Wars, 1996–2004" (Ph.D. diss., City University of New York Graduate Center, forthcoming 2006).

65. Human Rights Watch, *Casualties of War*.

66. Ibid., pp. 109–110.

67. Nest, "The Evolution of a Fragmented State," p. 295.

68. For information on private entrepreneurs and their links to ZANU-PF officials, see "Rhodies to the Rescue," *Africa Confidential* 40, no. 22, November 5, 1999, p. 6; "Soldiers of Misfortune," *Africa Confidential* 41, no. 18, September 15, 2000, p. 7; "Glittering Prizes II," *Africa Confidential* 41, no. 12, June 9, 2000, p. 8; "Glittering Prizes from the War," *Africa Confidential* 41, no. 11, May 26, 2000; John Matisonn, "Zimbabwe Top Brass Have Vested Interests in the DRC War," *Saturday Star* (Johannesburg), April 1, 2000, p. 5; David Furlonger, "Ventures into the Interior," *Financial Mail* (Johannesburg), May 28, 1999, pp. 58–60.

69. In a confidential interview with the author in March 2000, one Zimbabwean entrepreneur commented, "Things are normal somewhere like Kenya, but in the DRC we thought there would be no competition."

70. Several reports even cast doubt on the profitability of diamond ventures. See "Glittering Prizes from the War," *Africa Confidential,* p. 2; Vincent Kahiya, "No Diamond Cheques for Zimbabwe in the DRC," *Zimbabwe Independent* (Harare), March 10, 2000, p. 1.

71. See Mungbalemwe Koyame and John F. Clark, "The Economic Impact of the Congo War," in Clark, *The African Stakes of the Congo War*, p. 214.

Thomas Turner argues that the DRC government gave Sonangol-Congo control over the DRC fuel market as a reward for the FAA's support (see Turner, "Angola's Role in the Congo War," p. 87).

72. Ingrid Samset, "Conflict of Interests or Interests in Conflict? Diamonds and War in the DRC," *Review of African Political Economy,* no. 93/94 (2002): 475.

73. See United Nations, *Report of the Panel of Experts,* p. 28.

74. See Tim Raeymaekers, *Network War: An Introduction to Congo's Privatised War Economy* (Brussels: International Peace Information Service, 2002), pp. 21–22.

75. For example, Alfred Rwigema, son-in-law of Rwandan president Paul Kagame, was the DRC and Rwandan representative of a Dutch-American coltan trading firm. Cuvelier and Raeymaekers, *European Companies and the Coltan Trade,* p. 13.

76. For a discussion of the role of Congolese intermediaries, see Vlassenroot and Romkema, "The Emergence of a New Order?" p. 7.

77. Timothy Longman, "The Complex Reasons for Rwanda's Engagement in Congo," in John F. Clark, ed., *The African Stakes of the Congo War* (New York: Palgrave Macmillan, 2002), p. 137.

78. Cuvelier and Raeymaekers, *European Companies and the Coltan Trade,* p. 9.

79. Jake Sherman, "Burma: Lessons from the Cease-Fires," in Karen Ballentine and Jake Sherman, eds., *The Political Economy of Armed Conflict: Beyond Greed and Grievance* (Boulder, Colo.: Lynne Rienner, 2003), pp. 225–255.

80. Ibid., p. 247.

81. United Nations, (New York: UN, October 2002).

82. Van Acker and Vlassenroot, "Les 'Maï-Maï' et les functions de la violence milicienne dans l'Est due Congo," p. 108.

4

Economic Agendas in the Congolese Peace Process

François Grignon

Economic interests represent one of the most serious challenges to the Congolese peace process as well as for governance in general at the national and local levels. As argued in Chapter 2, these interests have deep historical roots in the DRC and have always posed challenges to peace and development. Despite progress in the political negotiations devoted to ending the Congo War, several brutal conflicts—including wars by proxy—that are at least partially fed by economic agendas continue in eastern DRC.

The challenge of the Congolese peace process is to lay the foundation for a state that will be rooted in national and local systems of good governance as well as provide for the security and prosperity of its neighbors. In light of this challenge, to what extent has the peace process been able to address the economic agendas of combatants and to provide for the economic well-being of the country as a whole? The question is important because the foundational peace instruments will shape economic governance in the posttransitional era. Can a successful long-term peace be created in a context of continuing violent competition over resources when other fundamental conflicts over citizenship, ethnicity, and security remain unresolved? More generally, when is it appropriate for peace processes to acknowledge and deal with economic interests, especially given that some parties will refuse to participate if economic interests are directly tabled and addressed?

This chapter explores these political and policy questions by analyzing the degree to which economic agendas have been incorporated into the peace processes associated with the Congo War, and by evaluating the initiatives the international community has taken to address such issues. Whereas Chapter 3 detailed some of the specific economic activities of belligerents, this chapter analyzes the military and political relationships that have facilitated the realization of these interests. I argue that Congolese domestic actors and the international community have only superficially viewed economic interests as a conflict issue. As a consequence, the solutions they have proposed for addressing the exploitation of resources suffer from a dramatic lack of credibility. But this does not mean that economic interests have been ignored. Indeed, economic interests have been *integrated* into the peace process and become a virtual "hidden script" whereby belligerents cooperated with each other and their foreign governmental patrons to protect and disguise their own and their patrons' economic interests. The rhetoric of transparency and equitable development was used to distract the Congolese public and donors and to disguise the belligerents' true intentions. Similarly, initiatives by the international community to promote or broker peace, as well as to publicize and prevent the illegal exploitation of resources and to develop alternative options for sustainable regional development, have lacked impartiality and been shaped by foreign governments' unspoken economic interests in the DRC.

Challenges of Peacemaking in the DRC

Almost a year and a half after the signing of the Lusaka Ceasefire Agreement in August 1999, the Congolese peace process finally began to register some significant progress. The key reason was the death of Laurent Kabila in January 2001, which created several new opportunities. Interstate fighting came to a halt, Rwandan and Ugandan troops withdrew from their advance positions, and the neutral facilitator appointed by the African Union (then the Organization of African Unity)—former Botswanan head of state Sir Ketumile Masire—began to organize an Inter-Congolese Dialogue (ICD) to create a "new political dispensation" for the DRC.[1] After some initial hiccups, the ICD convened in Sun City, South Africa, from February to April 2002, but did not immediately deliver the expected comprehensive political agreement necessary for the speedy establishment of a transitional government.

Progress was also made on the security chapter of the peace process. On July 30, 2002, the South African government persuaded the governments of Rwanda and the DRC to sign a security protocol whereby in return for a commitment from the Rwandan government to withdraw its forces, the DRC government promised to dismantle and disarm all former Forces Armées Rwandaises and Interahamwe on Congolese territory. Despite the fact that the DRC government did not fulfill its promises—and still had not in 2005, three years later—the Rwandan government has nonetheless withdrawn its troops from eastern DRC.[2] On September 6, 2002, the Angolan government brokered a similar deal between Kinshasa and Kampala that established a joint pacification committee for the troubled region of Ituri in northeastern DRC.

On December 17, 2002, after an additional six months of international pressure and shuttle diplomacy by both the UN special envoy to the ICD, Moustapha Nyasse (former Senegalese prime minister), and the South African government, the five parties to the ICD finally concluded in Pretoria an agreement on the organization of power sharing during the period of political transition. On March 6, 2003, a constitution of transition and a protocol on the reform of the security services (most significantly, the shape of the future national army) were agreed upon and these documents were ratified in the concluding session of the ICD, on April 2, 2003, in Sun City.[3]

Optimism generated by the progress in the peace process from 2001 to mid-2003 has had to be tempered by the ongoing situation on the ground. The DRC finds itself in a condition of neither war nor peace and is plagued by persistent intense local conflicts on parts of its territory. Although the interstate war involving direct confrontation between seven nations and their militaries is definitely over, two other dimensions of the war—local and national—remain unresolved. In some cases, these conflicts continue because they involve regional actors that did not participate in the peace accords and therefore have nothing to lose or gain by continuing to fight. In other cases, the rebel parties to the peace accords have ignored their commitments, or at the very least the rebel leadership that participated in the peace agreements has been unable to exercise effective lines of control throughout their organizations.

Serious challenges to the peace agreement in the form of local conflicts have erupted periodically. For example, Mai Mai fighters occupied Uvira in October 2002, and on the same day that the last protocols of the ICD were signed, the UPDF occupied Bunia—an event that illustrates the disconnection between the negotiation process and the new dynamics of conflict on the ground. One of the gravest breaches of the peace accords occurred when a dissident faction of RCD-Goma, led by Colonel Jules Mutebutsi and supported by General Nkunda (another RCD-Goma figure and the leader of the Eighth Military Region headquartered in Goma), claimed that the Tutsi population was facing genocide and occupied Bukavu for a week in early June 2004. The claim of threatened genocide was later discounted, and the troops of Mutebutsi and Nkunda retreated after a withdrawal plan was negotiated by the United Nations Observer Mission to the Democratic Republic of Congo (MONUC).[4] However, the occupation undermined the credibility of the MONUC—especially in the eyes of the Congolese public—which faced protest demonstrations in Kinshasa and was perceived to have "allowed" the occupation to happen by not having stopped it.[5] Another serious challenge occurred in December 2005 when dissident soldiers, mostly Kinyarwanda-speaking members of RCD-Goma, pushed the 126th brigade of the Congolese armed forces (FADRC) out of Kanyabayonga and seized several other towns in North Kivu, causing an estimated 30,000 civilians to flee. This event strained relationships within the transitional government between the RCD-Goma leadership and other parties, as well as between the transitional government and the Rwandan government, which was accused of having sent troops into the DRC to help the dissidents (a charge vehemently denied by the Rwandan government). Allegations about Rwandan troops operating in the DRC abound, with sporadic reports from NGOs, aid agencies, and civilians that they have sighted Rwandan regular forces on operations in Congolese territory. Definitive proof of such a presence came in March 2004 when "a MONUC patrol encountered Rwandan soldiers in North Kivu."[6]

These incidents—all bloody and causing great disruption and insecurity to civilians—demonstrate three key aspects of the Congo War. First, and as noted in the Introduction, it is more correct to talk of Congo *wars*, for there have been several conflicts occurring simultaneously in the DRC since the early 1990s. The Lusaka accords and ICD have addressed only the formal international conflict. Second is the ease with which some actors that are not part of the peace negotiations are able to bring the DRC back to the brink of full-scale civil and international conflict. It is only through a combination of donor pressure and the MONUC's strengthened commitment to rapidly deploy an armed response that these local conflicts have not broadened even further in scope. Third, economic interests continue to be only one dimension of the Congo War and associated conflicts. While the occupations of Uvira and Bunia were undoubtedly motivated by economic concerns (both towns are key trading posts), there is evidence that the occupations of both Bukavu and Kanyabayonga and its surrounds were primarily driven by security concerns (to be sure, predatory economic behavior, such as looting, also occurred[7]).

Analysts' initial assumptions that foreign belligerents were in the

DRC solely for security concerns—and would therefore be satisfied if these concerns were addressed in peace talks—have clearly proved false, for there is ample evidence that each and every local, national, and regional actor has developed an economic agenda. These interests are yet to be addressed by any of the peace negotiations. But security interests—especially those of Rwanda—have also not been addressed, and this has been one of the key reasons for the upsurge of violence in 2004. Together with economic interests, unresolved security issues are one of the major reasons the Rwanda government and military maintain their close networks to organizations and militias in eastern DRC.

There are, therefore, several major obstacles to securing sustainable peace in the DRC. First, there is the endless multiplication of the parties to the conflict. Since the signing of the Lusaka accords, the RCD has split at least five times, including twice after the ICD.[8] Mai Mai groups in particular have been subject to endless splits and alliances that have made them a very difficult phenomenon to apprehend and their participation in negotiated peace a genuine political problem. Second, regional tensions over ongoing centralized political domination by Kinshasa remain unresolved, although there is at least a public debate over whether a federal system is needed.

Third, and most important, after almost seven years of war, the official parties to the peace process continue to have deeply entrenched economic interests that are not being adequately addressed or openly acknowledged. Economic interests have also been uppermost in the minds of the official peacemakers, the South African government. In January 2004, President Mbeki traveled to the DRC as the head of a high-level business delegation, a visit that was repeated in April 2005 by a sixty-strong delegation headed by the trade and industry minister.[9] Other governments of the region (such as Zambia, Kenya, and Tanzania) have been deeply frustrated at having been sidelined from the negotiations and have consequently restored close political relations with the DRC government and intensified trade relations. It was probably inevitable that governments in the region would have economic interests in the DRC given the size of its market and its mineral deposits. However, that has not meant that those interests have been accepted without prejudice. Some regional governments' economic ambitions for the DRC have been perceived by other actors as threatening, and these disgruntled actors may be tempted to spoil good economic relations in the region through military disruption to trade or direct economic sabotage. The three Western nations closest to the DRC government and most involved in the country—Belgium, France, and the United

States—also have economic agendas. The DRC's reconstruction and rebuilding of its industrial mining capacity—which will most likely be financed by multilateral donors—represent lucrative opportunities for multinational corporations from these countries.[10] It is therefore not surprising that the governments of these three countries have created a role for themselves in the DRC peace process through traditional tools of diplomacy: the UN Security Council and a UN Observer Mission.

Regional actors receiving spoils from the Congo War rightly see some of these developments in the peace process—such as the involvement of the UN through the MONUC and multilateral donors' funding of reconstruction—as a political attempt by Western powers to regain control over the DRC's economy and to sideline their political profits. The danger lies in the possibility that if regional or Congolese actors believe that they may become the "losers" of an internationalized postconflict reconstruction effort, they may become the spoilers of peace building. Stephen Stedman's finding in his study on the implementation of peace agreements in civil wars remains depressingly relevant for the DRC:

> The greater the difficulty of the environment, the greater the likelihood that peace implementation will fail. The two most important environmental sources of failure are the presence of spoiler-factions or leaders who oppose the peace agreement and use violence to undermine it, and neighboring states that oppose the peace agreement and assist the spoilers.[11]

The DRC suffers from both of these ailments. One of the most important challenges of the peace process is to ensure that a sufficient number of important actors—and this might include national and foreign actors and signatories and nonsignatories of the Pretoria power-sharing agreement—stand to gain something from a return to peace, and that these actors are institutionally able to prevail over those who stand to lose.

Unfortunately, the peace process largely ignores or has sidelined economic interests. The participants in the ICD have not thoroughly addressed the economic dimensions of the conflict and refuse to acknowledge any responsibility in the illegal exploitation of natural resources. These same parties have passed resolutions promising good economic governance and economic transparency that have still not been implemented. In other words, a "fool's game" has been played by participants in the ICD and now by the transitional government, who pretend to support radical reforms in the management of the DRC's state and economy while simultaneously working hard to ensure that no international guarantees are set up to verify compliance with their own commitments. Despite three relatively well-documented reports published by the UN Panel of Experts on the Illegal Exploitation of Natural Resources and Other Forms of Wealth of the Democratic Republic of Congo, many belligerents still bluntly dismiss as irrelevant the illegal exploitation of resources that occurred during the Congo War. In particular, from the point of view of the governments of Rwanda, Uganda, and Zimbabwe, economic agendas are simply not, nor have they ever been, an issue. They have held consistently to the view that their involvement in the DRC conflict has been driven by concerns about security and sovereignty, and nothing else.[12]

Western powers have not been any more transparent in this respect. The permanent members of the UN Security Council who established the UN panel—France, the United Kingdom, and the United States—never intended to have a frank and open debate about the economic agendas surrounding the conflict. This is because they often preferred political expediency to any acknowledgment that their own multinational corporations were deeply involved in the licit and illicit exploitation of DRC's natural resources. Once opened, the "closet" of illegal economic exploitation of the Congo has revealed the ugly head of militarized mercantilism.[13] However, it was opened by Western governments only in order to put political pressure on the more obvious regional beneficiaries of the conflict—Rwanda, Uganda, and Zimbabwe—whose governments were identified by the UN Panel of Experts as the primary obstacles to the peace process when its investigation was launched in June 2000. Western governments have been extremely reluctant to acknowledge their own responsibility for the conflict, either in the origins of the war (through their sustained support to the Mobutu regime) or the role of European- or North American–based transnational corporations in exploiting resources and in exacerbating the conflict.

These challenges have made efforts to strengthen the peace process a difficult and politically fraught process. How can the challenges posed by economic interests be addressed if those interests are not publicly acknowledged? The peace agreements continue to be regarded by many as suspect, containing hidden agendas, and are considered unlikely to make a difference on the ground. The provisions of the agreements are seen as torn between rival solutions for regional political and economic problems. Eventually, economic agendas will have to be addressed if an end is to be found to conflict in the Great Lakes.

It will probably be the responsibility of the donor community, through "aid for peace" bargaining mechanisms, to discipline the actors involved in the transition and to freeze foreign aid to regional spoilers. These arrangements will give donor organizations a real chance to make a difference to the prospects for the region, but there are complications. Donor governments have economic—and political and security—agendas in addition to their aid agendas. Because of the power and influence of business interests within Western governments, it is highly unlikely that the economic agendas of Western governments will be made secondary to aid agendas or even temporarily shelved. The Congolese government's efforts to liberalize the economy and attract Western capital (see Chapter 3) also suggest that it accepts and hopes that donor countries will continue to be economically involved in the DRC. The solution is for donor governments to be open about their economic interests, and in this respect they could probably learn something from the South Africans. But they should also work together to create a joint, multi-track, peacebuilding strategy that lays the foundation for better patterns of governance in the DRC (including their own role in such patterns) and better options for sustainable development for the Great Lakes region.

Economic Agendas from Lusaka to Pretoria

The Lusaka Ceasefire Agreement—or Lusaka accords or agreement—is the central pillar of the peace process in the DRC. It was signed in August and September 1999 after a year of difficult negotiations between Laurent Kabila and the two rebel groups that led the war, the RCD and the MLC. The agreement was facilitated by South Africa and, in particular, by Zambia (then chair of the Southern African Development Community's defense and security committee). The agreement consists of two security chapters and a political section. The two security chapters address the withdrawal of foreign troops (Chapter 4) and the disarmament of "negative forces" (Chapter 9), that is, Rwandan ex-FAR and Interahamwe, Ugandan Allied Democratic Forces (ADF), the West Nile Bank Front (WNBF), the Burundian Conseil National de la Démocratie–Forces de Défense de la Démocratie, and Angolan UNITA. The political chapter recommended an Inter-Congolese Dialogue organized by a neutral facilitator, followed by the establishment of the new political dispensation for the DRC that would lead to the organization of national elections in June 2005 (subsequently delayed).

The inclusion of such aspects into the Lusaka accords did not stop the war. Rather, it froze the military frontline that stretched across the country and allowed Laurent Kabila to consolidate the FAC's defenses in the face of a threatened RPA advance on the diamond town of Mbuji-Mayi that would have cut the links between Kinshasa and Lubumbashi. Had this offensive been successful, it would probably have resulted in the total defeat of the FAC.[14] The DRC government's signing of the Lusaka accords can therefore also be viewed as a strategic maneuver designed to buy the government time to improve its military position.

While the Lusaka accords allowed the Kabila regime to survive militarily, they represented a serious political defeat for Laurent Kabila personally. For one year Kabila had consistently refused to meet with rebel leaders, agreeing only to talk to foreign "aggressors" (i.e., the Rwandan and Ugandan governments), but the agreement forced him to both meet with rebel leaders and publicly acknowledge his loss of control over half of the DRC's territory.[15] In addition to giving official recognition to the two rebel groups, the Lusaka agreement also forced Laurent Kabila to participate in a dialogue where opposition political parties and civil society representatives hostile to his government were given equal status with the three main belligerents (the DRC government, the RCD factions, and the MLC), which resulted in Kabila sharing power. The hostility of these civilian actors toward Kabila was largely the result of his own actions, for after adopting repressive policies on civil and political liberties, he had made enemies of groups that had formerly opposed Mobutu and probably should have been his natural allies.[16] Kabila was hence forced to enter political negotiations with four opponents.

The Lusaka accords were primarily a ceasefire agreement aimed at guaranteeing a permanent suspension of hostilities. Security and political issues dominated the negotiations and economic agendas were not considered relevant to the peace process. At the time of its signing, evidence had already been mounting that all belligerents were actively involved in the exploitation of resources.[17] However, the parties to the agreement considered these activities to be a by-product of war and a secondary matter that should not have an impact on the course of the peace process. By establishing the legitimacy of rebel organizations' claims to power, the Lusaka agreement legalized the partition of the country into three distinct zones and enabled the rebels to legitimately claim that they both officially represented their part of the country and had the authority to administer and exploit their zone. Economic agendas remained publicly unacknowledged until the UN Security Council created its Panel of Experts on the Illegal Exploitation of Natural

Resources and Other Forms of Wealth in June 2000—after the third battle in Kisangani between Rwandan and Ugandan troops.

The Inter-Congolese Dialogue

The organization of the ICD—the only forum where economic agendas
were able to be raised under the Lusaka agreement—did not move forward until the death of Laurent Kabila. Kabila had first tried to manipulate the process in his favor, reportedly by offering Ketumile Masire, the
neutral facilitator for the ICD, U.S.$1 million if he could "guarantee that
he was selected as interim president of the transitional arrangement to
emerge from the ICD."[18] Having failed to do that, he then did everything he could to delay its implementation. Despite his obfuscations, the
Joint Military Commission created by the Lusaka agreement managed to
produce two military disengagement plans (signed in Harare and
Kampala) and clarified the respective defensive positions of the belligerents. However, the ICD remained paralyzed. While Kabila initially
accepted Ketumile Masire, he later consistently opposed and humiliated
him and did everything he could to prevent both a genuine power-sharing agreement and any focus on the economic dimensions of the conflict.[19] It was not until preparatory talks in Gaborone, Botswana, in July
2001, that economic issues were finally incorporated into the official
agenda of the ICD.

Following Laurent Kabila's death in January 2001 and the ascendancy of his son, Joseph Kabila, to the presidency, the peace process
accelerated. The progress was almost entirely the result of Joseph
Kabila's interest in peace, although he also benefited from Western
donors being receptive to dealing with someone new. On his first day in
office, he publicly announced his intention to relaunch the peace
process, and one month later he announced he would cooperate with
Masire to restart the ICD.[20] These actions suggest that Joseph Kabila's
interests were somewhat different from those of his father, but precisely
why Joseph Kabila has been so interested in peace remains unclear. One
possibility is that proclaiming his support for the ICD was a strategy to
consolidate his power both domestically (among a Congolese public and
civil society sceptical of his suitability for the presidency) and internationally (among donors sceptical of his ability to lead the government
into a peace agreement).

By July 2001, Masire had managed to jump-start the ICD by organizing a preparatory meeting in Gaborone with representatives of the five
parties—the DRC government, RCD, MLC, political opposition, and

civil society—to agree on its framework and on its agenda. It was at the Gaborone preparatory meeting that the exact composition of the delegations, including how the churches, other civil society representatives, the Mai Mai, the political parties and rebel groups split from the original RCD would be represented, was to be determined.[21]

In April 2001, two months before the Gaborone meeting, the publication of the first report of the UN Panel of Experts that had brought attention to the exploitation of resources organized by Rwanda and Uganda, was received in Kinshasa with a nationalistic outcry. The government's own involvement in the looting, in collaboration with Zimbabwean actors, was overlooked. The impact of the report was that economic interests could no longer be ignored by parties to the peace process. The four main Congolese belligerents signed the Declaration of Fundamental Principles of the Inter-Congolese Political Negotiations on May 4, 2001, in Gaborone. Article 11 of the declaration proclaims "the utilization of the natural resources of the Democratic Republic of Congo in the interests of the whole country and for the improvement of the living standards of the Congolese people."[22] The facilitators argued that economic issues were an essential item that should be placed on the official agenda of the dialogue, and all parties subsequently agreed to the creation of an Economic and Financial Commission within the framework of the talks. The final communiqué of the meeting even produced a "Republican Pact" to be immediately respected by all the signatories who committed themselves to a "return without condition all properties illegally acquired or requisitioned" (Article 3.6) and to "protect the national heritage and resources against all forms of looting" (Article 3.8).[23] Point 8 of the draft agenda of the dialogue also mentioned a "review of the content and validity of the economic and financial conventions signed during the war"[24]—a review that has now been completed by the transitional government. In sum, *on paper* the issues of theft and other forms of illegal exploitation of national resources were to be addressed by the ICD and would benefit from the immediate implementation of the Republican Pact. In practice, the commitments made in Gaborone have never been implemented.

Even if the Congolese belligerents had actually wanted to adhere to their signed commitment—which is doubtful—their regional backers would not have allowed it. For example, Joseph Kabila flew to Harare during the talks to explain the intended "review of the economic and financial conventions signed during the war" and to provide guarantees that the Zimbabwean interests would remain untouched.[25] Any decisions made by the DRC government also had to be "confirmed via phone calls to Kinshasa and then to Harare and back to Gaborone."[26] A recurrent political dynamic of later meetings of the ICD emerged at this point: eager to gain the support of civil society delegates and to consolidate their democratic and good governance credibility in the eyes of the Congolese public, the three belligerents committed themselves to standards of political accountability and economic transparency that they had no intention of respecting. The ICD thus became a forum in which the belligerents give testimonies as to their good faith and credible intentions regarding the reconstruction of a better Congo, but these testimonies are never matched by deeds. And this has subsequently been the case, as is evidenced by the absence of any concrete actions by members of the transitional government to alter patterns of economic behavior or reallocate or return assets.

In Gaborone, the battle over the final composition and number of delegations to attend the talks could not be resolved. The conflict over the composition of the civil society and political party delegations was still unresolved when facilitators called for the opening of the Addis Ababa meeting in October 2001. The inability of the delegates to resolve this issue led to the quick collapse of the talks. The Kinshasa government, afraid of being sidelined by the RCD-MLC alliance, abruptly refused to discuss any issue of substance and quit the Addis talks using the pretext of incomplete representation of the interested parties. The composition of the two other delegations was the focus of a battle between the various belligerents who attempted to increase their control over the deliberations by influencing which political party leaders, civil society representations, and Mai Mai delegates attended the meeting. A deal was finally brokered, with the help of the UN special envoy Ibrahima Fall, in December 2001, and the South African venue of Sun City was accepted for the forty-five-day consultations to be started on February 25, 2002.[27]

The *Addendum* to the UN Panel of Experts' first report, released in November 2001, put the spotlight on Kinshasa's own complicity with Zimbabwean actors in the exploitation of resources and was consequently met with little enthusiasm by Congolese government officials. Like the first report, however, the *Addendum* was met by a national outcry from the Congolese public that could not be ignored. Politicians who hoped to present themselves to the Congolese electorate after a short transition were forced to show that they were somehow committed to end their predatory behavior.

The Fourth Commission of the ICD, presided over by Albert

Trevoedjre from Benin, was devoted to economic and financial issues, with five economically related items on the commission's official agenda: (1) a review of the validity of the economic and financial conventions signed during the war; (2) an inventory of the destructive acts that occurred during the war and the identification of those responsible for them; (3) an evaluation of the cost of the two wars; (4) an emergency economic and social program of reconstruction; and (5) the return of the properties stolen from private parties and other assets requisitioned from the state.[28] In accordance with the first item on the agenda, a resolution was proposed recommending the establishment during the transition of an ad hoc parliamentary commission to look into all the contracts signed by the belligerents with foreign companies during the two wars (an activity that was completed in May 2005).[29] The proposed resolution also laid out terms of reference for this commission of inquiry.[30]

Despite such far-reaching resolutions, the economic dimensions to the war never became issues for real debate at the ICD, for attention and effort remained centered on the political and security commissions, where power sharing was supposed to take place. This was because the outcome of the power-sharing agreement would determine the organization of national resource sharing—not resolutions from the Fourth Commission, which were mainly public relations exercises in response to either the UN Panel of Experts' reports or attempts by delegations to restore some credibility to their economic management (which they knew would determine the conditions of international aid flows).[31] Some delegations were openly unconcerned about either good governance or public relations and opposed the resolution's implementation.[32]

On the political front, the Sun City talks delivered only a partial agreement between Joseph Kabila and Jean-Pierre Bemba. The talks confirmed the former as the president of the transitional government and provided the latter with the post of prime minister. However, the Sun City agreement collapsed two months later when, during the writing of a constitution of transition (in Matadi, DRC, from June 6 to July 5, 2002), the government started to question the powers devolved to the prime minister's office and the MLC questioned the government's insistence that it be in sole control and command of the national army.[33] The agreement was further undermined when the RCD-Goma launched the Association for the Salvation of the Dialogue (ASD) with political parties—such as Etienne Tshisekedi's Union pour la Démocratie et le Progrès Social (UDPS)—to oppose the Sun City deal. The ASD collapsed by the end of May 2002 after a mutiny within RCD-Goma forces in Kisangani was brutally repressed, leading to the extrajudicial killings of hundreds of civil society representatives, as well as other civilians who had demonstrated their support to the mutineers or who were caught in the cross fire. In the face of such repression, ASD members were unable to sustain their public opposition.

In July 2002, the UN secretary-general appointed a special envoy, Mustapha Nyasse, to help restart the dialogue and finalize the political chapter of the talks. Nyasse, who had chaired the political commission at Sun City, began rounds of shuttle diplomacy between the belligerents to broker a new political deal. By the beginning of November 2002, representatives of the five parties to the dialogue were brought back to South Africa to start a final round of talks over power sharing. After more weeks of negotiations and great pressure being placed on the delegations by all the countries of the region (especially by the governments of Gabon and Congo-Brazzaville on the MLC), a political agreement—the All-Inclusive Agreement on the Transition in the Democratic Republic of Congo—was finally signed on December 17, 2002.

The December 17 Agreement

The December 17 Agreement is aimed at distributing positions in the institutions of transition between the three belligerents and two unarmed components of the ICD. Joseph Kabila—or, rather, his political party, Parti pour la Reconstruction et le Développement (PPRD)—retains the position of head of state, and four vice-presidencies were created for the government, the RCD-Goma, the MLC, and the unarmed opposition.[34] The program of the transitional government is based on the resolutions adopted at Sun City. The legislative branch of government is composed of a 500-member National Assembly and a 120-member Senate, shared among the five ICD components. An Implementation and Monitoring Commission (IMC) was also created to help with the interpretation of the agreement, resolve any conflict, oversee the power sharing at the provincial level, and decide on the nominations of ambassadors and other members of the government. The IMC is assisted in its conflict resolution role by an International Committee that supports the implementation of the program of transition. In the agreement, no mention is made of the MONUC, the United Nations at large, or the African Union. The Congolese negotiators obviously preferred to have minimum international interference in the management of the transition and in the implementation of the Sun City resolutions.[35]

The final chapter in the negotiation process closed on March 6,

2003, when a security chapter on the reform of the security services (including the future national army) and a Constitution of Transition was agreed upon. The ICD finally concluded with a special session back in Sun City on April 2, 2003. At the session, all documents adopted on March 6, 2003, were endorsed and signed under the terms of the December 17 (2002) Agreement—although the DRC government noted that the Mai Mai and RCD-ML "signed with reservations."[36] Implementation of the major aspects of the peace agreement unfolded over the next five months, including the official introduction of the transitional constitution (April 4); the swearing in of Joseph Kabila as president of the transitional government (April 7); the signing by belligerents of a memorandum on the restructuring and integration of the army (June 29); the swearing in of vice presidents, ministers, and vice ministers over the month of July; and the official inauguration of the Senate and National Assembly on August 22.[37]

The December 17 Agreement and the program of transition commit the signatories to ending the illicit exploitation of natural resources, *on paper*. Measures include the previously mentioned review of contracts and regular financial audits. But two factors should temper enthusiasm for these commitments. First, despite such agreements, the same patterns of exploitation of natural resources continued unabated in 2002—even while the agreements were being negotiated—and have continued right through to 2005.[38] Even if they wanted to become transparent in their economic activities—which they do not—transparency would endanger relations between Congolese belligerents and their regional governmental patrons and the commercial networks that link them. The fear of Congolese belligerents was that foreign allies might not continue providing military and political support, jeopardizing their economic interests.[39]

Second, the economically related guarantees included in the December 17 Agreement have been undermined by the scope and structure of the agreement's instruments. The IMC is exclusively composed of, and run by, the signatories, and no Congolese or other external party has any role in monitoring what the IMC actually does (the International Committee charged with helping the IMC will, at best, have an advisory role). During the last phase of negotiations in Pretoria, the Congolese parties unanimously refused any external interference in their implementation of the agreement, and as a result the IMC has no authority to demand answers from the government or investigate whether the commitments made on paper really are being implemented. In short, there are absolutely no guarantees that any of the promises made regarding good economic governance in the program of transition or the power-sharing agreement will be implemented. As all decisions within the government and at the IMC are made by consensus, and as virtually all parties are equally culpable, it is unlikely that any party will ever be accused of violating the agreement on economic grounds.

Addressing Economic Interests

The argument that the peace process has not addressed economic interests is strengthened by an analysis of different actors' primary interests and motivations to continue fighting. The ICD, which is currently the sole mechanism for dealing with economic issues, operated under the assumption that the five participating parties are the only actors that should decide the DRC's economic and political future. The reality is that other actors—excluded from the ICD—continue to shape the DRC's future.

During the peace negotiations and prior to their incorporation into the transitional government, the MLC and RCD at times behaved simply as proxies of regional players—i.e., neighboring governments—and had little independence. Indeed, they even appeared to negotiate on behalf of their regional backers as much as for themselves. Clearly, the most militarily, politically, and economically powerful actors of the war—regional governments—were not party to the dialogue and were even able to dismiss individual leaders of their Congolese partners in favor of more compliant ones.

Furthermore, because the ICD is based on the Lusaka agreement—which provides the legal basis for the peace process and remains the framework of reference for the peace process—the ICD is frozen in a system of power relations that has changed considerably over the course of the conflict. In particular, powerful domestic actors operating in eastern DRC—such as Ignace Murwanashyaka (leader of Rwanda's FDLR, composed of ex-Interahamwe now based in the DRC), Colonel Jules Mutebutsi (leader of the dissident RCD-Goma faction that participated in the occupation of Bukavu in June 2004), Colonel Nakabaka (former commander of a Mai Mai militia on the Rusizi Plain, South Kivu), Patrick Masunzu (leader of the Banyamulenge insurgency), and Thomas Lubanga (Hema-Gegere leader of the Union des Patriotes Congolais)—are not part of the transitional government and have been excluded from formal negotiations or, in the case of Mutebutsi, have by their actions deliberately placed themselves outside the process. They remain outside the process despite the fact that they hold key positions on the ground and clearly have the power to derail the peace—as evidenced by the fact that they have done so. At some stage, a mechanism that includes these actors in the negotiations will need to be established. To be sure, neither the ICD delegations nor the transitional government can be expanded indefinitely, but some kind of mechanism is still required to deal with such actors—certainly the Sun City resolutions are incapable of doing so. In the Kivus and Ituri, in particular, there appears to be an unlimited supply of opportunistic community leaders and local organizations ready to rebel against the peace agreement and the authority of the transitional government, as well as to seek benefits through the commercial and military networks founded and maintained by Rwandan and Ugandan forces. Domestic actors such as these are well placed to spoil the peace, undermine the transitional government, and further derail the already delayed elections.

Rwanda

Following the Sun City negotiations, the notion that Rwanda might regain complete control of the Kinshasa government's security services was definitively buried.[40] The Ugandan-engineered agreement between the DRC government and Jean-Pierre Bemba's MLC decisively sidelined the Rwandan government from having any role in the political settlemen—and illustrated Yoweri Museveni's influence on the peace process. The Pretoria and Luanda agreements of July and August 2002, confirmed Rwanda's growing isolation. Through the signing of these separate security agreements sponsored by South Africa and Angola, Joseph Kabila succeeded in sidelining the rebel movements and reintroducing the primacy of interstate logic for resolving the most important dimension of the DRC's conflict.

Yet, Joseph Kabila failed to meet his part of the deal. For example, instead of disarming and disbanding the FDLR—something the Kabila government was possibly also unable to do—the FDLR was allowed to consolidate its position in the Kivus, where it joined with other Rwandan expatriate militias hostile to the Kagame government and intensified its destabilization campaign against Rwanda. Following efforts by the Kabila government in 2002 to cut off its supply of weapons, the FDLR was weakened. However, 8,000 to 10,000 FDLR members continued to operate in eastern DRC as of 2005, and these forces have come to present one of the most serious challenges to civilian life and the peace process.[41]

To deal with this ongoing security concern, Kigali's only realistic option has been to maximize its influence in the Kivus. To this end, the Rwandan government has progressively relegated the national RCD leadership to a secondary tool of influence in Kinshasa and focused instead on creating and strengthening autonomous power bases in the areas of the DRC it considers to be within its sphere of influence. In North Kivu, for example, it developed a two-pronged strategy. First, the Rwandan government has given Congolese Hutu community leaders preeminent positions in the provincial administration to reduce their temptation to join the DRC-based Hutu forces seeking to attack Rwanda. For example, Eugene Serufuli, a former executive member of the Congolese Hutu self-help organization Mutuelle Agricole des Virunga (MAGRIVI), succeeded Gafandi Kanyamuhanga as governor of North Kivu in December 2000. Serufuli has led the campaign to co-opt his community leadership into the RCD. Former Congolese Hutu fighters were also recruited en masse into the military wing of the RCD.[42] Second, Rwanda tightened its surveillance and control over Rutshuru. From early 1999, non-*génocidaire* ex-FAR soldiers were transferred from the Rwandan army into the RCD's forces to train, recruit, and supervise Local Defence Forces (LDF) units in Rutshuru. Demobilized Hutu soldiers from the Rwandan army and LDF from Rwanda were also regularly transferred to Rutshuru.[43]

Governor Serufuli of North Kivu now also heads Tous pour la Paix et le Développement (TPD), a parastatal NGO directly linked to the Rwandan Directorate of Military Intelligence, that was established soon after the RCD itself. The TPD was designed to complement counterinsurgency activities by implementing local development projects that address some of the socioeconomic grievances of the local population. In North Kivu the TPD functions as an alternative political authority that vets all appointments within the territorial administration, including the RCD's military arm. It is the backbone of the governor's authority in the province, right down to the lowest levels, and was involved in transporting troops to Bukavu during the occupation of that town by dissident RCD-Goma troops.[44] Serufuli is reputed to have a small army of 10,000 to 15,000 troops, independent from the RCD's high command but closely linked to the Rwandan leadership.[45] A similar pattern of troop transfers under the guise of humanitarian or developmental activities also occurred in Masisi. In June 2002, the TPD repatriated by force up to 9,500 Congolese Tutsi refugees from camps in Byumba and Kibuye provinces in Rwanda to Masisi. The U.S. Committee for Refugees reported that "the forced repatriation from Kiziba (one of the two Congolese refugee camps in Rwanda) was done, at least in part, to provide cover for return of the demobilised-Rwandan soldiers to Eastern DRC" and to "develop an ethnic Tutsi constituency in Eastern DRC, from which, in part, to recruit young men into armed militia."[46]

There is strong evidence that these tight security arrangements aimed at preventing FDLR infiltration are also linked to an economic project to reestablish cattle ranching—an activity that was once profitable but was destroyed during the 1990s. For example, up to 28,000 head of cattle were transferred from the Gishwati forest to the Kililorwe area of Masisi.[47] Some of these cattle allegedly belonged to the Rwandan and RCD Tutsi establishment and benefited from the armed protection provided by LDF units as part of their general security responsibilities in North Kivu. As reported by the UN's *Final Report* in October 2002, Rwanda was also strongly suspected of trying to build in North Kivu, under the RCD umbrella, autonomous power bases that would have stronger political and economic allegiance to Kigali than to Kinshasa. The Rwandan government's methods include entrenching a permanent and efficient surveillance system, notwithstanding the withdrawal of its troops under the Lusaka accords, and pursuing the quiet but highly lucrative administration of all available economic resources, regardless of the commitments made under the peace agreement. In such a context, it will be extremely difficult for any central authority in Kinshasa to regain administrative control of the DRC's eastern periphery. On the basis of their effective territorial control, autonomous forces allied to Rwanda that were not party to the Pretoria power sharing agreement will always be in a position to reject the outcomes of this agreement.[48]

A similar dynamic is taking place in South Kivu. The Rwandan government's plan to strengthen autonomous tendencies in South Kivu is motivated by both security concerns and its willingness to continue exploiting resources regardless of the resolutions of the ICD. From mid-2002, the Rwandan government began negotiating separate deals with Mai Mai leaders to prevent any grand Congolese alliance that would support the FDLR and to consolidate Rwandan control over the exploitation of the Kivus' resources.

The Rwandan government, in need of strategic allies for its military operations in the Kivus against the FDLR, sponsors autonomous movements and offers to share resources and power with local leaders independently of political relationships in Kinshasa. The Kivus have therefore become an ideal terrain for the multiplication of Congolese armed groups driven in particular by their desire to control coltan and diamond mines—economic behavior which, with the connivance of Rwanda, has repeatedly brought the peace process to the brink of failure.

Uganda

The interests and strategies of the Ugandan government are different from those of Rwanda. Kampala no longer faces any significant security threat from eastern Congo, but the evidence suggests that it seeks to maintain a sphere of influence over Orientale province and northern parts of North Kivu. Such an arrangement would ensure that Ugandan army commanders continue benefiting from the exploitation of natural resources that they began following the UPDF's occupation of the DRC. In support of this goal, the Ugandan government tried to create a confederation of allies, led by Jean-Pierre Bemba, that would guarantee the security of Uganda's interest over Congo's territory.

Throughout 2000, Uganda sought to reconcile its Congolese proxies. It recreated a joint political movement within its sphere of influence in Equateur and Orientale provinces: the Front de Libération du Congo (FLC). The FLC was to unite Jean-Pierre Bemba (MLC) and three RCD factions headed by Wamba dia Wamba (RCD-K), Roger Lumbala (RCD-National), and Mbusa Nyamwisi (RCD-ML), but it failed miserably. Bemba, the designated FLC leader, came to Beni-Butembo at the beginning of 2001 to try to pacify the region and rally local Mai Mai leaders. A short-lived ceasefire agreement was signed on March 29, 2001, with some North Kivu Mai Mai leaders, but others remained either independent or allied themselves with rival rebel leader Mbusa Nyamwisi.[49] Bemba never honoured his commitment to pay, arm, and train his new Mai Mai allies, hence the collapse of the limited agreement barely two weeks after it was signed. After Bemba arrested RCD-ML officers and attempted to transfer their troops to Equateur, direct confrontations erupted in June 2001 between the Mai Mai, Nyamwisi's militia, and the MLC inside the towns of Beni, Butembo, and Lubero. Soon after, the FLC completely collapsed. Helped by the UPDF, Nyamwisi subsequently tried to establish his authority in Beni and Lubero, but he never received popular support, largely because of the taxes his group levied on cross-border trade to and from Uganda.[50] The scope and depth of Nyamwisi's control over these areas has continued to fluctuate depending on his capacity at any one time to co-opt or coerce local Mai Mai groups, as well as to control the exploitation of the local gold and coltan mines by striking business deals with his Ugandan military allies.[51]

In the wake of the failure of the FLC, Bemba urgently needed to increase his bargaining capacity for the final sessions of the ICD—basically through proving that he controlled a sufficiently largely proportion of Orientale province and was therefore a force to be reckoned with. RCD-National leader, Roger Lumbala, who controls only the diamond-producing area of Bafwasende, became instrumental in this quest of Bemba's and offered a perfect alibi to attack the RCD-ML and take control of the significant amount of territory within the province that it controlled. At the end of October 2002, fighting erupted between the RCD-National and the RCD-ML in Ituri—it is unclear if this was deliberate provocation as part of the Bemba-Lumbala plot—and Bemba sent his troops to "rescue" RCD-National forces, quickly moving to occupy the eastern town of Mambasa. Nyamwisi's RCD-ML received military support from the DRC government and successfully resisted the MLC-RCD-National military offensive. In January 2003 in Gbadolite, the MONUC managed to broker a ceasefire agreement between all parties. Bemba welcomed the negotiations but agreed to participate only as an observer. The ink had barely dried on this agreement when fighting resumed and the MLC advanced eastward again, causing massive suffering and dislocation of the civilian population.

All the actors in these developments in Orientale province have, at one time or another, been political and economic allies of the Ugandan government. In fact, the Ugandan government continues both to supply them with weapons and ammunitions and to participate in the marketing of natural resources they have exploited. The relationships and behaviour of actors in this Uganda-orchestrated situation are driven by political and economic motives. Neither Kampala—nor Kinshasa—has an interest in seeing Jean-Pierre Bemba or Mbusa Nyamwisi become too powerful in Orientale province, hence the support they provide on a regular basis to breakaway factions and various ethnic leaders.

Community and ethnic-based aspirations for territorial and resource control have created powerful incentives for rebel groups to reject any power or resource sharing with leaders coming from other communities, as well as to create new armed movements.[52] In addition to their use of extreme violence on civilian populations and very weak chains of command and hierarchical authority, some of these groups suffer from a repetitive and endless process of fragmentation that represents a genuine threat to the peace process. The evidence suggests, however, that such "chaos" is, in fact, carefully orchestrated and managed instability—that is, "organized chaos"—and is symptomatic of the influence the exploitation of resources has on those rebel groups that have no agenda other than economic gain and access to local or national positions of power for predatory reasons. Of course, some rebel groups have extensive political interests and do not fall into this category.

Zimbabwe

Harare's economic interests appear to be less destructive for the peace process than the interests of the Rwandan and Ugandan governments. Zimbabwean interests are unlikely to cause renewed fighting or endanger the continued implementation of the peace agreement. But Harare's loss of political influence in Kinshasa during 2002 does not mean that Zimbabwe's ambitions vis-à-vis the DRC's resources have disappeared. Throughout the talks, Harare's two key Congolese frontmen in Kinshasa—the DRC government's hard-liners Mwenze Kongolo and Augustin Katumba Mwanke—were obstacles to the talks' progress or success. Every time these two government ministers arrived in South Africa for the negotiations, the talks suffered a setback. It was not until they were dismissed from the government—following the public outcry at the UN's final report, which revealed Kongolo's and Mwanke's involvement in the illicit exploitation of natural resources—that the negotiations were able to be finalized.

After Sun City, the Zimbabwean government approached Kinshasa to ensure that its interests were not at risk. A number of contracts were renegotiated and signed anew, with the understanding that they would not be subject to any kind of review by any parliamentary commission. Furthermore, while the Zimbabwean army entirely withdrew from the DRC, several Zimbabwean generals created private security companies that remain in charge of surveillance at diamond concessions controlled by Zimbabwean interests. These companies play the same role as the ZDF had prior to its withdrawal. Given the severity of Zimbabwe's own economic crisis, it is highly unlikely that the Zimbabwean government would undertake any action that might jeopardize these assets or the willingness of the Kabila government to repay its political debt to Harare. At the beginning of 2003, the Zimbabwean government began to press Joseph Kabila to repay some of the approximately U.S.$220 million it had spent in military support of the DRC government.[53] This unpaid debt remains a contentious issue.

The UN Panel of Experts and the International Conference on the Great Lakes

Two instruments have been established by the international community to deal with the economic dimension of the Congo War: (1) the UN Panel of Experts on the Illegal Exploitation of Natural Resources and

Other Forms of Wealth of the Democratic Republic of Congo; and (2) the UN mandate provided to a special representative of the secretary-general based in Nairobi for the preparation of the International Conference on Peace, Security, Democracy, and Development in the Great Lakes Region. The mandate was first held by Ambassador Berhanu Dinka, followed by Ambassador Ibrahima Fall. The MONUC was established to support the implementation of the Lusaka agreement and has no relation whatsoever with the two other UN instruments. Its role was conceived of as a minimalist answer to the needs of the peace process, yet support even for this has been lacking—especially from the U.S. government, which did not want to commit itself politically or financially. Washington feared that given the lack of commitment on the part of the Congolese parties, any large-scale operation would be extremely expensive and have little chance of success. The U.S. government agreed to the establishment of the MONUC only on the condition that the United States could both determine its operational scope and limit its mandate to the strict minimum of a phased deployment leading to ceasefire violation observation and voluntary disarmament, demobilization, repatriation, resettlement, and reintegration (DDRRR) programs for the different foreign rebel groups.[54] The UN panel and the Great Lakes conference mandates were issued totally independently from the MONUC's activities.

The UN Panel of Experts: Political Expediency and Half Solutions

The panel was created in the wake of unresolved tension between the Security Council, Rwanda, and Uganda. For months the Security Council had urged—with no effect—that the Rwandan and Ugandan governments demilitarize Kisangani in the wake of clashes there between their respective militaries in the first half of 2000. During a visit in early May 2000 to the Great Lakes region, representatives of the Security Council, led by France, raised the issue of illegal exploitation of resources with the actors of the peace process and recommended that an expert panel be established to investigate the matter. A month later, following the outcry that unfolded after the Kisangani fighting, the president of the Security Council asked the UN secretary-general to proceed with the establishment of a panel to investigate the illegal exploitation of natural resources in the DRC. The panel was to be established for a period of six months, with the following mandate:

> To follow up on reports and collect information on all activities of ille-
> gal exploitation of natural resources and other forms of wealth of the
> Democratic Republic of Congo, including in violation of the sover-
> eignty of that country; To research and analyse the links between the
> exploitation of the natural resources and other forms of wealth in the
> Democratic Republic of Congo and the continuation of the conflict; To
> revert with the Council with recommendations.[55]

The French government, in particular, had wanted an international
instrument to put pressure on Rwanda and Uganda and to weaken their
international credibility by proving that both countries were occupying
the DRC not so much for security reasons as for economic reasons. The
French government was the only permanent member of the Security
Council that was very interested in the Congo War and, as a result of its
interest, it was informally granted a leadership position on the issue by
the other permanent members.[56] The French ambassador to the UN,
Jean-David Levitte, had led the Council's visit to the Great Lakes and
provided the recommendation that was endorsed in June 2000.

From the beginning, the panel received an unofficial mandate by
France to be heavily critical of Rwanda and Uganda. The uncompromis-
ing stance of the two countries and the continuing military threat they
represented to Kinshasa was perceived by the French as one of the key
problems of the peace process, hence the necessity of finding an angle
through which political pressure could be levied. Throughout its initial
investigation, the Quai d'Orsay facilitated the panel's work and the
French intelligence services even provided some of the incriminating
information regarding Rwandan and Ugandan participation in the illegal
exploitation and trade in DRC's resources.[57] At the behest of the French
government, the panel decided that Kinshasa's involvement in the
exploitation could not be investigated since the government was the
internationally recognized holder of state authority and because
Zimbabwe's troops were officially invited to the DRC. As a result, the
legitimacy and credibility of the first report of the panel was undermined by its inherent bias against Rwanda and Uganda.

The publication of the first *Report of the Panel of Experts* created
an uproar that the French government could not control. Its bias in favor
of Kinshasa and its attempt to directly incriminate Yoweri Museveni and
Paul Kagame and their coteries was perceived as gross political manipulation and backfired. Its recommendations, however justified, were dismissed as politically motivated. Indeed, some of them *were* politically
motivated—such as the proposals to embargo Congolese coltan, freeze
rebel assets, and withhold budget support from regional governments

involved in the coltan trade. This proposal was directly aimed at financially strangling Rwanda, Uganda, and their allies in order to weaken them or push them out of the DRC. The report also paid little heed to the consequences that would have resulted had its recommendations been implemented. For example, an embargo on coltan would have been a disaster for the Kivutien population given that coltan mining is critical to the livelihood of the region. Clearly, the panel had sought to establish that the continuation of the war was economically motivated and therefore came to conclusions that were preordained.

Regardless of the value of the information presented in the report, it was rejected in total by the Rwandan and Ugandan governments. In fact, while the report was an embarrassment for these governments, its lack of political credibility—as a result of its perceived bias—meant that it had little capacity to pressure these governments to cease their military and economic activities in the DRC. Pressured by London and Washington, Paris agreed to an addendum to the report that would serve to balance the UN's analysis of the illegal exploitation of natural resources by concentrating on the activities of Zimbabwe and individuals in the Congolese government.

Washington was also uncomfortable that U.S. officials and companies had been incriminated by early drafts of the report. The economic section of the U.S. embassy in Kigali had been extremely active at the beginning of the war in helping to establish joint ventures to exploit coltan, but the initial draft of the report was edited to remove any mention of the role of the U.S. government or firms in the conflict, in order to avoid embarrassing the U.S. government.[58] As a result, only Africans were incriminated, and the names and activities of Western companies and individuals—which were responsible for much of the exploitation, marketing, processing, and consumption of natural resources—were largely omitted.[59]

The *Addendum to the Report*, published in November 2001, downplayed the controversial recommendations that had been issued in the first report: the request for an embargo on coltan exports was transformed into a moratorium, the withholding of direct budget support by international financial institutions was suggested as an alternative option, and the recommendations of sanctions were even lifted. However, due to divisions within the UN—particularly between France and the UK (which defended Rwanda and Uganda and rejected all conclusions against them)—the Security Council did not take any action. The international community was left with a confused situation. While the UN panel had exposed a key issue of the Congo War, the international community failed to take any credible action in response because of political expediency and divisions among Security Council members. In lieu of action, the Security Council in effect commissioned a third report with a mandate to balance and strengthen the analysis of the reporting and to provide a set of recommendations that would present a credible way forward for the DRC.

The third and final report is the most credible, balanced, and thorough work of all the Expert Panel reports. It contains original information on the exploitation carried out by all actors and includes an attempt to refine a framework of analysis with which to characterize the patterns of exploitation (that is, the "elite network" concept that is used by all three reports to describe the association of individuals—Congolese and non-Congolese—involved in the illegal exploitation of natural resources). The panel was again given an unofficial "attack Rwanda" mandate by the French, but the *Final Report* went far beyond this. Its most controversial recommendations—the travel ban and the freezing of assets of a list of individuals and companies—were far more balanced than the initial versions and gave Joseph Kabila the ideal pretext to temporarily suspend some of his government hard-liners, including Mwenze Kongolo and Augustin Katumba Mwanke, an action that boosted the credibility of the DRC government in the peace negotiations. These figures have subsequently returned to elite political circles.

The panel's attempt to make a strong case regarding the illegal exploitation of natural resources was challenged by the swift withdrawal of the Rwandan army and most other foreign troops from the Congo. The end of direct foreign occupation seemed to discredit the initial charge of the panel: that the continuation of the war and the occupation of the DRC by foreign troops were economically motivated. The elite network concept partly answered that challenge, as it clearly indicated that the exploitation of resources could continue to the benefit of foreign interests, even after their troops were withdrawn. By taking this approach, the *Final Report* simultaneously brought back to the center of analysis and discussion the role of Congolese actors, including their own contribution to the continuation of the conflict, the kind of state that needs to be reconstructed in the DRC, and the composition of any resource-sharing agreement within that state.

The recommendations of the *Final Report* began to address these issues, but they did so neither decisively nor comprehensively. The *Final Report* failed to offer a conclusive policy framework for managing the exploitation of natural resources from a strictly Congolese, regional, or international point of view. Part of the problem lies with the mandate of the panel itself. The panel was conceived as a means of applying pressure on foreign belligerents and not as an entry point into the Congo peace and reconstruction process, which remains closely guarded by regional actors.

In its conclusions, the panel made a brief reference to the other international tool to be created by the UN Security Council to deal with long-term economic and security issues in the Great Lakes: the International Conference on Peace, Security, Democracy, and Development in the Great Lakes Region. It noted that "such a conference would be an ideal forum to address the need to reorient the regional trading system to post-conflict imperatives and for negotiating the framework of multilateral agreement to carry this out."[60] However, an examination shows that it is unlikely that such a conference could address or change the Congo's pattern of economic governance.

The International Conference: Part of the Solution?

The idea of an international conference to guarantee the long-term stability of the Great Lakes region dates back to the AFDL campaign against the Mobutu regime. The intertwining of several national conflicts in Uganda, Rwanda, and Angola with the collapse of the Zairian State led many observers to believe that only a regional approach could produce long-term solutions to these problems. The idea of an international conference was initially circulated by the French—partly as a means of recovering its role as a power broker in the region after its diplomatic debacle in the Rwanda genocide—and has circulated in diplomatic circles ever since. At the end of 1999, soon after the signing of the Lusaka agreement, the UN secretary-general took a first step to operationalize the idea and mandated the special representative based in Nairobi to produce a concept paper and a roadmap for the conference. However, from day one the UN faced hostility from several governments that suspected that any attempt to hold an "international" conference was a ploy by Western governments to steal the initiative from regional governments, and by the end of 2000, the idea of a concept paper had been shelved. During its second visit to the Great Lakes, the Security Council, led by France, reintroduced the idea but this time circulated a "nonpaper" on the matter.[61]

The ability of an international conference to resolve some of the problems linked to the exploitation of resources is not clear from the nonpaper. By laying out the broad framework for an initiative to be taken by the African Union with the support of the UN, and addressing three dimensions of the Great Lakes crisis (security, democracy, and sustainable development), the conference is designed to bring regional governments together to sign a number of protocols and agreements on all issues related to peace and security.[62] Yet how and when issues raised in the conference would be addressed remains unclear. The nonpaper also does not address the compatibility between this initiative and other African initiatives that are devoted to peace, stability, and sustainable development, such as the South African–sponsored New Partnership for African Development (NEPAD). Most importantly, it does not take into consideration the fact that the countries of the region do not have a uniform understanding of democracy and sustainable development. The Rwandan and Ugandan leadership, in particular, have disputed the suitability of multiparty democracy for their own countries and give different justifications for the control or containment of press and political party activities. Finally, it is necessary to inquire whether Congolese actors are prepared for, and can contribute to, such a conference.

The governments of Rwanda and Uganda continue to argue that such a conference would be premature until a viable transitional government is in place in the DRC, and the fundamental security origins of the conflict—for Kigali, in particular, the disarmament of anti-Rwandan government forces based in the DRC—have been successfully addressed. For both Kigali and Kampala, discussions regarding the long-term consolidation of peace and security in the Great Lakes can only occur when a permanent and satisfactory solution has been found to the Congo War, and it is their belief that such a conference would distract attention from this core issue.[63] Both governments have long perceived the proposed conference as a deviation from the Lusaka agreement and its focus on their security concerns. The Rwandan government especially fears involvement by all regional governments, as the governments of the Republic of Congo, the Central African Republic, and Tanzania are hostile to Rwanda, a situation that would increase the likelihood of the latter's political isolation. Without an initial consensus between the signatories of the Lusaka agreement on basic issues such as timing, framework, objectives, agenda, and the expected outcome of the conference, as well as some coordination with other initiatives such as NEPAD, it is likely that many commitments will be made at a proposed conference, but few actions will result.

There is one ready option for making the conference relevant in the DRC, and that is to use it to launch a permanent conflict prevention and resolution mechanism that would address cross-border sources of destabilization and economic integration.[64] As such, the conference could build peace and facilitate postconflict stabilization throughout the Great Lakes, as well as consolidate the DRC peace process. However, until security issues are resolved to the satisfaction of most governments in the region, it is unlikely that any agreement will be reached on the establishment of a permanent regional security mechanism.

Conclusion

The economic interests of various actors in the DRC are not merely foreign creations sustained through economic or political domination on the part of expatriate actors. Congolese actors and their interests have become deeply embedded in the criminal, violent, and inequitable exploitation of natural resources. This has also been the case with the peace process. Participants feared their own criminal economic behavior would be exposed if economic issues were placed on the agenda and that they would be forced to give up some of their economic activities as a result. To be sure, the manipulation of the peace process by Congolese belligerents was partly at the command of their foreign governmental patrons, but it was also a function of domestic autochtonous attempts to secure private and organizational economic advantage.

Thus have all peace instruments created since the Lusaka accords referred to economic issues and called for an end to predation, illegal exploitation, and corrupt government, but actual implementation of these arrangements has never included any serious attempt to address real economic issues. In fact, economic issues have been separated from political agendas. This has enabled parties to make empty promises to address the former, while allowing them to continue exploiting natural resources while first resolving political and security issues.

The international community's role in the peace process has also been steeped in hypocrisy. While criticizing the economic behavior of Congolese actors and the governments of Rwanda, Uganda, and Zimbabwe, and applying pressure on these actors, Western donors— especially the governments of France, the United States, and the United Kingdom—have simultaneously attempted to disguise the deep involvement of their own countries in the exploitation of natural resources, as revealed by their attempts to determine the focus of the three reports of the UN Panel of Experts. The official peace broker, the South African government, has been less hypocritical in that its business delegations have been highly public and—being headed by the president—clearly linked to the political establishment. However, the South African government has remained coy about admitting that its pursuit of a role in the DRC peace process was driven, possibly primarily, by the interests of the business community.

Does this mean that peace brokers should have tried to put economic interests squarely and publicly on the negotiating table and tried to simultaneously address economic, political, and military concerns? In the case of the Congo War, the answer to this question is not clear. Several parties would undoubtedly have refused to participate if economic interests had been directly tabled, resulting in even more prolonged and wider-ranging conflicts than currently exist in the Great Lakes region. Given that economic interests cannot be ignored if long-lasting peace is to be achieved, the question therefore arises as to when economic, political, and military interests should be introduced and addressed in peace processes. Specifically, when should this have occurred in the DRC peace process? The answer, which cannot be explored here, involves understanding the optimal sequence in which different interests could have been brought to the table, as well as a willingness to accept in the short term what should normally be unacceptable behavior in the interests of long-term peace. The cost of the peace agreement that is in place is a negative peace—actually, no peace at all in much of eastern DRC—that leaves most grievances and structural opportunities for economic predation intact.

Neither economic issues neglected by the peace process nor the continuing surreptitious realization of economic interests by participants are the only reasons that conflict continues to flare in the DRC. The structure of the ICD itself has become an obstacle to peace. While the ICD has been, and remains, critical to implementing peace in the DRC, the system of power relations that produced the ICD—and that is perpetuated by it—hampers efforts to build peace. The explanation is that although the political and military relations between all the parties involved in the conflict continued to evolve from 1998 to 2005, the ICD remains frozen in the system of relations that existed midconflict and that does not offer the flexibility needed to address ongoing security and economic concerns. Peacebuilding at the national level and the creation or reorganization of posttransitional institutions must be linked to peace efforts for eastern DRC. Continuing dialogue over postconflict political arrangements must recognize that all nonsignatories to the Lusaka agreement and all nonparticipants to the ICD are potential spoilers of both the transition and its peacebuilding initiatives on account of both economic and security interests. Given this, peace negotiations for eastern DRC—

where important nonsignatories and nonparticipants are concentrated— must address outstanding economic and security grievances, as well as hasten the implementation of demobilization and disarmament programs and the creation of alternative livelihoods for combatants.

Notes

1. See Article 19 of the Lusaka Ceasefire Agreement. The text of the agreement is available on the website of the Office of the Facilitator for the Inter-Congolese Dialogue (OFICD), www.drcpeace.org,

2. The Rwandan government has threatened to return troops to the DRC if the MONUC fails to halt cross-border attacks by the FDLR into Rwanda. While President Paul Kagame denies this has already occurred, in 2004, the MONUC began to find circumstantial evidence that suggested that small numbers of Rwandan troops were in the DRC ("U.N. Sees 'More and More' Signs that Rwandan Troops Are in Congo," Associated Press, December 3, 2004).

3. Paule Bouvier, in collaboration with Francesca Bomboko, *Le dialogue intercongolais: Anatomie d'une négociation à la lisière du chaos; Contribution à la théorie de la négociation* (Tervuren, Belgium: Institut Africain–Cedaf, 2003), pp. 263–267.

4. Stephanie Wolters, "Continuing Instability in the Kivus: Testing the DRC Transition to the Limit," Occasional Paper No. 94 (Pretoria: Institute of Strategic Studies, 2004).

5. See International Crisis Group, *Back to the Brink in the Congo*, Africa Briefing No. 21 (Nairobi: ICG, December 17, 2004).

6. Wolters, "Continuing Instability in the Kivus," p. 7.

7. Ibid., p. 3.

8. Since all fifty founding members of the RCD are signatories of the Lusaka Ceasefire Agreement, they could all be legally entitled to separate representation in the peace process, including the ICD.

9. Zimbabwean government officials suspect that the South Africa government offered to mediate the peace process in order to obtain an "entry ticket" for the South African private sector to the DRC markets and natural resources— an economic ambition Harare deeply resents (author's interview with Zimbabwean official, May 2001). President Mugabe even refused at first to allow the DRC government to agree to any rounds of talks being held in South Africa, although this was probably also related to his perception that doing so would give the RCD an advantage (the South African government had a close relationship with Rwanda, and Mugabe feared that this would give the RCD an advantage against the DRC government). Shelley Whitman, "Balancing Act: An Insider's View of the Inter-Congolese Dialogue," *African Studies Review* 12, no. 4 (2003): 133.

10. Since the signing of the Sun City agreement, representatives of the French and Belgian trade chambers have visited Kinshasa, calling for the immediate resumption of international aid to the Congolese government. Reconstructing roads and railway lines, revamping the Inga dam and its region-

al power grid, and distributing water are—among other projects—likely targets of European multinational corporations, which often rely on their respective government's political influence to win public tenders advertised by the DRC government. In 2000, MLC representatives also toured European capitals to talk business, indicating that domestic actors are also cognizant of the potential benefits from establishing economic ties to Western countries.

11. Stephen J. Stedman, "Implementing Peace Agreements in Civil Wars: Lessons and Recommendations for Policy Makers" (New York: International Peace Academy, May 2001), p. 2.

12. See, for example, "Reaction of the Government of Rwanda to the Report of the Panel of Experts On the Illegal Exploitation of Natural Resources and Other Forms of Wealth of the Democratic Republic of Congo," (Kigali, August 26, 2001), available at www.rwanda1.com/government/04_22_01news_Response_To_UN_Report.htm.

13. Chris Dietrich, "The Commercialisation of Military Deployment in Africa" (Pretoria: Institute for Security Studies, January 26, 2001).

14. Emile Havenne, "La deuxième guerre d'Afrique centrale," in Filip Reyntjens and Stefaan Marysse, eds., *L'Afrique des Grands Lacs, Annuaire 2000–2001* (Antwerp: Centre d'Étude de la Région des Grands Lacs d'Afrique, 2001), pp. 143–174.

15. International Crisis Group, *The Agreement on a Cease-fire in the Democratic Republic of Congo: An Analysis of the Agreement and Prospects for Peace*, DRC Report No. 5 (Nairobi: ICG, August 20, 1999).

16. Gauthier de Villers, Jean-Claude Willame, Jean Omasombo Tshonda, and Eric Kennes, *République démocratique du Congo: Chronique politique de l'entre-deux-guerres, Octobre 1996–Juillet 1998*, Cahiers Africains 35–36 (Tervuren, Belgium: Institut Africain–Cedaf, 1998).

17. An example of economic interests that came to light during the negotiations themselves was the battle between Rwandan and Ugandan troops for the control of Kisangani that erupted in May 1999. A shaken Wamba dia Wamba, the initial leader of the RCD, went to Lusaka in June 1999 convinced that the Rwandans had attempted to kill him in Kisangani during the battle in order to establish full control over the rebel movement and the town's diamond market. Two subsequent battles between Rwandan and Ugandan troops over Kisangani were similarly politically and economically motivated by their desire to control the province's diamond markets. See International Crisis Group, *Uganda and Rwanda: Friends or Enemies?* Africa Report No. 14 (Nairobi: ICG, May 4, 2000); ICG, *Rwanda/Uganda: A Dangerous War of Nerves*, Africa Briefing (Nairobi: ICG, December 21, 2001).

18. "Whitman, "Balancing Act," p. 134.

19. International Crisis Group, *Scramble for the Congo: Anatomy of an Ugly War*, Africa Report No. 26 (Nairobi: ICG, December 20, 2000).

20. Kevin Dunn, "A Survival Guide to Kinshasa: Lessons of the Father Passed Down to the Son," in John F. Clark, *The African Stakes of the Congo War* (New York: Palgrave Macmillan, 2002), p. 69.

21. International Crisis Group, *Le dialogue intercongolais: Poker menteur ou négociation politique?* Africa Report No. 37 (Nairobi: ICG, November 16, 2001).

22. Declaration of Fundamental Principles of the Inter-Congolese Political Negotiations, available at the website of the Office of the Facilitator for the Inter-Congolese Dialogue, www.drcpeace.org, p. 2.

23. Office of the Facilitator for the Inter-Congolese Dialogue, *Communiqué final des travaux du pré-dialogue,* Gaborone, 2001.

24. Office of the Facilitator for the Inter-Congolese Dialogue, *Draft Agenda of the Inter-Congolese Dialogue,* Gaborone, 2001.

25. Author's interview with an adviser to President Joseph Kabila, August 2001.

26. Whitman, "Balancing Act," p. 133.

27. International Crisis Group, "Storm Clouds over Sun City: The Urgent Need to Recast the Congolese Peace Process," Africa Report No. 44 (Nairobi: ICG, March 14, 2002).

28. Bureau d'Études, du Recherche et du Consulting International, *Rapport d'évaluation: 7ème semaine du Dialogue Intercongolais* (Kinshasa: BERCI, April 8–14, 2002).

29. The official objectives of the commission's inquiry were: to establish an inventory of all the conventions signed between the 1996 and 1998 wars; analyze these conventions; establish the financial impact of these conventions; validate or reject these conventions; and demand possible reparations in favor of the DRC.

30. The proposed terms of reference were: respect of the principles of sovereignty and territorial integrity of the DRC; respect of the legal texts and regulations organizing the specific economic sector; respect of the signatories' competences; respect of the principle of nonillicit acquisition of wealth; consideration of the reports issued by the UN panel on the illegal exploitation of natural resources and other forms of wealth in the DRC; consideration of the consequences on the population; obligation of transparency in the procedures leading to the signing of the said conventions; and legal presentation of the conventions within the necessary time frame imposed on the signatories (Bureau d'Études, du Recherche et du Consulting International, *Rapport d'évaluation*, p. 7).

31. Author's interview with Inter-Congolese Dialogue delegates, Sun City, April 2002.

32. For example, the MLC and the RCD-National officially registered in the report of the commission that they had never signed any economic or financial conventions. The RCD-ML added that the contracts it signed should not be reviewed (Bureau d'Études, du Recherche et du Consulting International, *Rapport d'évaluation*).

33. United Nations Office for the Coordination of Humanitarian Affairs–Integrated Regional Information Networks, "DRC: Talks on Transitional Government Stall over Army" (Geneva: OCHA, July 9, 2002).

34. The civil society component was not allocated a vice presidency, but it obtained two ministerial positions, three assistant minister positions, and the chair of the five institutions dedicated to the democratization of the country: the National Electoral Commission, the Higher Authority on the Media, the Truth and Reconciliation Commission, the National Human Rights Commission, and the Commission on Ethics and the Fight Against Corruption. Each vice presi-

dency is responsible for overseeing an Executive Commission which will coordinate the activities of the relevant ministries. The RCD received the Political Commission; the Economic and Finance Commission was given to the MLC; the Commission for Reconstruction and Development was given to the government; and the unarmed political opposition received the Social and Cultural Commission. The armed parties and the unarmed oppositions also each received seven ministerial positions and four assistant minister positions. In addition, the RCD-ML, the RCD-National, and the Mai Mai received two ministerial and two assistant minister positions each. Members of the government are also forbidden to buy or rent either directly or indirectly any property belonging to the state. It will be mandatory for members of the government, when taking and leaving office, to submit to the National Assembly a written declaration of their properties. See the facilitator's *Final Report for the Inter-Congolese Dialogue* at www.drcpeace.org.

35. A number of provisions were included to try to both limit personal enrichment by individual members of the transitional institutions and guarantee the transparency of the management of key state assets, such as mining parastatals. For example, Annex 2 (devoted entirely to parastatals) stipulates the following: all appointments to executive and board positions will have to be reviewed by the government, which will ensure that the holders of these positions have the necessary expertise and a university degree; all parastatals should work under the close supervision of the relevant government department and their finances will be audited every six months by independent firms, with audits then being presented to the government and tabled in the National Assembly for approbation; each parastatal should register any conflict of interest arising from the activities of its executives, and a code of ethics will have to be followed by all employees; and salaries and staffing of parastatals must be approved by the transitional government. (See *Accord global et inclusif sur la transition en République démocratique du Congo*, Pretoria, 2002). While these statements seem practical and useful, the transitional government's limited capacity to verify or monitor parastatals makes it unlikely that they will ever be enacted or enforced.

36. Bouvier, *Le dialogue intercongolais*, p. 271.

37. Ibid., p. 303.

38. For example, the "Republican Pact" signed in Gaborone was supposed to be implemented immediately after the preparatory meeting of the talks, but no action followed. In another example, while the Economic Commission was preparing its resolutions in Sun City, the head of the National Intelligence Agency (*Agence Nationale de Renseignements*, ANR), Didier Kazadi Nyembwe, was negotiating secret contracts with South African investors (author's interview with ICD delegate, Sun City, April 2002). Kazadi Nyembwe was later identified by the UN Panel of Experts' *Final Report* as one of the main culprits of the illegal exploitation of resources among Kinshasa officials.

39. See International Crisis Group, *Storm Clouds over Sun City;* International Crisis Group, *The Kivus: The Crucible of the Congo Conflict,* Africa Report No. 56 (Nairobi: ICG, January 24, 2003).

40. Part of this section was previously published by the author in *The Kivus,* ibid.

41. International Crisis Group, *Pulling Back from the Brink in the Congo*, Africa Report No. 91 (Nairobi: ICG, March 30, 2005).
42. African Rights, *DRC: The Cycle of Conflict; Which Way Out in the Kivus?* (London: African Rights, December 2000).
43. Author interviews with RCD officials, Goma, DRC, November 2002.
44. Wolters, "Continuing Instability in the Kivus," p. 4.
45. Aloys Tegera, *Grands lacs africains et perspective* (Goma, DRC: Pole Institute, October 4, 2002).
46. Joël Frustone, "The Forced Repatriation of Congolese Refugees Living in Rwanda" (Washington, D.C.: U.S. Committee for Refugees, December 16, 2002).
47. Author's interview with Eugène Sérufuli, Goma, DRC, October 2002.
48. Aloys Tegera, *Nord-Kivu: Une rebellion dans la rebellion?* (Goma, DRC: Pole Institute, March 2003).
49. Integrated Regional Information Networks, "DRC: Bemba-Led Rebel Group Signs Accord with Mayi Mayi," March 29, 2001.
50. Author's interviews with Congolese traders in 2001.
51. For more details see Human Rights Watch, *Chaos in Eastern Congo: U.N. Action Needed Now* (New York: HRW, October 2002); "Congo-Kinshasa: Soldiers Go, Plunderers Stay," *Africa Confidential* 43, no. 21, October 25, 2002; Dominic Johnson, *Shifting Sands: Oil Exploration in the Rift Valley and the Congo Conflict* (Goma, DRC: Pole Institute, March 2003).
52. For example, in Ituri, the RCD-ML of Mbusa Nyamwisi was created from a secession of Banande and Bahema leaders of the RCD who hoped to control North Kivu and the eastern part of Orientale province. Thomas Lubanga seceded from the RCD-ML to support his Hema-Gegere supporters' ambitions to control the Kilo Moto gold mines. Simultaneously, neighboring ethnic Lendu and Ngiti militias were created by alternative leaders to oppose such ambitions. In North and South Kivu, a similar spiral of ethnic community-based insurgencies and resistance against foreign (i.e., non-Congolese and non-local) occupation has fed the Mai Mai dynamic. All these actors are likely spoilers of the peace process.
53. "Government Presses DRC to Pay $100 bn in Debt in Forex," *Financial Gazette* (Harare), January 9, 2003. One hundred billion Zimbabwean dollars were converted to U.S. dollars at U.S.$1= Z$456.
54. See International Crisis Group, *Scramble for the Congo*.
55. United Nations Security Council, press release SC/6871, June 2, 2000.
56. France obtained support for its leadership position on the Great Lakes from the United States and the United Kingdom in exchange for French support for other international crises closer to these two countries' core political interests, such as in Sudan, Sierra Leone, and Liberia.
57. Author's interview with French government official, December 2001.
58. Author's interview with panel member, May 2001.
59. All references to U.S. interests were withdrawn, and only a few British and German companies were mentioned as importers of coltan. A French multinational, Bollore, was heavily involved in the transport of the resources from the Kenyan port of Mombasa to Europe, but this fact was also ignored (ibid.).
60. United Nations, *Final Report*, paragraph 160, pp. 29–20.

61. A nonpaper is a document circulated by one or several members of the Security Council that has not been officially endorsed as a Security Council document.

62. These issues include respect for and control over borders; security and defense policy; confidence-building and conflict-prevention measures; arms movements in the region; democracy, including the promotion of democratic institutions and the rule of law; promotion of and respect for human rights and basic freedoms; protection of minorities and refugees; promotion of reconciliation and prevention of discrimination, ethnic violence, and genocide; reconstruction and development, including transparent and macroeconomic policies, promotion of trade and investment, transborder cooperation, and regional integration; reconstruction and modernization of public administrations; poverty reduction policies; and environmental protection.

63. Author's interviews with Rwandan and government officials, Kigali and Kampala, 2001.

64. In this respect, the conference could function along the lines of the Organization for Security and Co-operation in Europe.

5

Legacies of the War Economy: Economic Challenges for Postconflict Reconstruction

Emizet F. Kisangani

In February 2002, the South African government began hosting peace talks to resolve the Congo War—or what many commentators have called Africa's "First World War." Despite the talks culminating in the peace agreement and the formation of a Government of National Unity and Transition in mid-2003, building and sustaining peace in the Democratic Republic of Congo remains a daunting challenge. Some key problems are that security of people and property is yet to be achieved, and militia groups continue to terrorize the local population and target reconstruction efforts, UN peacekeepers, and foreign companies investing in the DRC.[1] The World Bank is candid about the economic fragility of the DRC, estimating that it will take fifty-six years for the DRC to reach 1960 levels of gross domestic product (GDP).[2] The IMF has predicted that it will take forty-five years for the DRC to reach levels of development present in 1990[3]—a year when mineral processing and exporting from Katanga provided a substantial contribution to national coffers.

The transition remains susceptible to collapse because the Inter-Congolese Dialogue process has addressed neither the economic dimensions of local conflicts nor the sharing of political power at the local level. This is because the peace process has concentrated on bringing an end to hostilities at the inter-state and national levels and was deliberately vague about the underlying economic factors of the conflict. Furthermore, "spoiler elements" of the transitional government, which have nothing to gain from elections, continue to threaten to pull out of the transition, leading some analysts to fear for the future of the current process.[4]

By several measures, the DRC represents a highly difficult environ-

99

ment for successful peace implementation. Georges Downs and Stephen Stedman have shown that factors mitigating against successful peace implementation include state collapse, the existence of more than two belligerent groups, the presence of armed combatants that number over 50,000 soldiers, the presence of hostile neighboring states or regional networks, and the existence of disposable natural resources.[5] *All* of these conditions obtain in the DRC and together increase both the opportunities and the incentives for one or more former rebel or belligerent groups to engage in peace-spoiling behavior. The postconflict environment in the DRC, and the Great Lakes region more generally, is also complicated by the fact that many ordinary citizens have become dependent on the war economy—even though it impoverishes the majority, displaces millions of people, and transforms patterns of land ownership in favor of those who control instruments of violence.

Ongoing insecurity and patterns of economic behavior created by the war economy have produced serious obstacles to the implementation of disarmament, demobilization, repatriation, resettlement, and reintegration (DDRRR) programs and the restoration of good economic and political governance. Under these conditions, "winning" the peace will be at least as difficult as securing peace accords, because breaking the violent and criminal dynamics of the war economy will require considerable resources and tightly focused strategies. As is the case for the other difficult postconflict environments of the 1990s and 2000s, successful postwar reconstruction in the DRC requires international implementers to provide "greater amounts of financial resources, risk more peacekeepers, and pursue more coercive strategies than those associated with traditional peacekeeping."[6] Unfortunately, there is little indication that the international community will devote the resources necessary for success. A key problem is that reconstruction programs address the current causes of economic malaise, but they do not address the causes of the conflict.

This chapter has three purposes. Drawing on Amartya Sen's "entitlement approach," it first identifies the legacies of the war economy and the challenges they pose to peace implementation and reconstruction. I argue that there are three main economic legacies of the conflict: new patterns of economic ownership, an interruption to subsistence agriculture, and confused property rights. Second, I evaluate the reconstruction programs being implemented by four multilateral agencies: the United Nations Mission in the Democratic Republic of Congo (MONUC), the United Nations Development Programme (UNDP), the World Bank, and the International Monetary Fund (IMF). I argue that while these programs have made some important achievements, their design contains significant flaws and their implementation remains fraught. I also analyze new regulatory frameworks introduced to facilitate reconstruction by creating better conditions for investment and production in the natural resources sector. Finally, I argue that if postconflict reconstruction is to be truly successful, reconstruction programs need to address additional specific issues related to the economic reconfiguration that occurred during the Congo War.

Legacies of the War Economy

A useful way to understand the human impact of the legacies of the war economy is to analyze their effect on human capital, especially on "entitlements." Entitlement relates to what Sen calls the "acquirement problem" and refers to all forms of legal income—that is, all forms of legal acquirement—from work, assets, and transfers.[7] An entitlement *approach* "focuses on the forces that determine the bundles of commodities over which a family or an individual can establish command."[8] An entitlement approach is a useful way to capture the impact of the war economy on citizens because of the importance of farmers' food production in exchange and in agricultural waged labor. Food production has an immediate relevance for the entitlement of farmers who try to acquire as much food as possible by growing food in order to trade or to exchange surplus for nonfarm products.[9] In this regard, the price of food provides a major linkage between production and entitlement and hence the to exchange entitlement of those who rely on market purchases to meet their food requirement. Food and nonfood agricultural production also shape demand for agricultural waged labor, through which many Congolese earn cash. Fluctuations in wages and employment in agriculture are therefore important factors in determining the entitlements of agricultural laborers. Laborers and their families can be reduced to misery if a change in either the endowment or exchange entitlement makes it no longer possible to acquire a commodity bundle that contains sufficient food. Although production and entitlement are conceptually distinct categories, the causal link between them is strong enough to create a close positive association between the two. This close association derives from the preeminent role that food crops occupy in Congolese life.

There is overwhelming evidence that war destroys and inflicts huge costs on both subsistence farmers and waged labor, and thus on society in general. Entitlements are destroyed when armed groups seize control over resources, and do so by using coercion (rather than payment or exchange). The destruction also extends to the entitlements of educated and professional groups—a key part of any society's human capital—as well as women, who constitute the majority of the workforce in subsistence economic activity in Africa. During war, wealth and power subsequently become dependent on, and are generated by, the coercive control of rents from resources, and transfers to and within armed groups and their supporters.

In the case of the DRC after 1999 when the frontlines of battle became relatively stable, communities in territories held by antigovernment forces were particularly badly affected. Because rebel groups were not interested in maintaining even the most basic public health or social services, families that had had their entitlements destroyed were virtually unable to obtain services of any kind. Families in government-controlled territory also saw their public entitlements reduced. Government spending on education increased from 0.83 percent of combined military and presidential spending in 1998 to 2.8 percent in 1999, only to drop back to 0.91 percent in 2000.[10] Health spending and other social services also suffered, and there has been a decline in expenditure on public works, which plummeted from 9.4 percent of military and presidential spending in 1999 to 1.78 percent in 2000. An examination of public and social spending as a percentage of total spending reveals that between 1998 and 2000, public entitlements were reduced by almost 37 percent.[11]

In addition to the destruction of entitlements, the Congo War has also caused the reconfiguration of patterns of economic control. There have been two distinct trends. First, there has been a trend toward ethnic-based control in territory held by antigovernment forces. This is an extremely sensitive issue because of its ethnic dimension and one that the ICD and donors have not tackled. For example, several ethnic groups, such as the Hunde, were reported to have been killed in North Kivu by Hutu militias—the same militias that usually left Congolese (Kinyarwanda-speaking) Hutu unharmed after robbing them. In the case of Hunde miners, those who managed to escape from Hutu militias became victims of the Tutsi-dominated RPA and the Banyamulenge- and Banyarwanda-dominated RCD militias, while Banyamulenge and Banyarwanda civilians were protected by Tutsi soldiers.[12] Indeed, there has been extensive collaboration between Banyamulenge and Banyarwanda and Rwandan forces. The reorganization of the economy of eastern DRC along ethnic lines—especially the control and production of lucrative minerals—poses many challenges for resolving the ongoing violence and for postwar reconstruction.

Second, the oligarchic control of resources that occurred in the Belgian and Mobutu eras has been retained, but in government zones a newly wealthy oligarchy has come to monopolize the exploitation of resources and has displaced old elites. Many top-level government officials and their associates have accumulated great wealth, which they could not have done in the absence of the war. This has occurred because of their control over instruments of violence, which has enabled them to illegally extract resources for their personal benefit with impunity.

It is particularly interesting to examine economic elites' reconfiguration of smuggling and other informal economic activities, because doing so gives an insight into the pervasiveness of the new oligarchy's economic interests across both formal and informal activities. But first it is worth emphasizing important differences between the informal economy in times of war and peace. Unlike war economies, informal economic activities in peacetime are not necessarily predatory or coercive. Activities undertaken outside the official economy are often highly productive and have important welfare benefits for the rural and urban poor in settings where the state is unable to extend them any benefits. In the DRC, the gains from illegal trade were captured by local communities or intermediaries who built and maintained civil entitlements, such as public schools and even roads. Illegal trade even came to be a form of political and economic resistance that enabled many to flourish at the expense of Mobutu's predatory state.[13]

In contrast to previous eras, and as discussed in earlier chapters, the anti-Kabila war has allowed networks of elites (especially military elites in eastern DRC with close links to Rwanda and Uganda) to capture the informal economy, radically transforming the survival strategies and wealth-generating smuggling activities that previously existed. The transformation occurred because the war forced the informal market—and informal operators—to behave according to the rule of those who controlled instruments of violence, including shifting price differentials to benefit the latter. In eastern DRC, Ugandan and Rwandan-dominated networks came to monopolize the market by subjecting the population to trade restrictions and by fixing prices. This has destroyed local traders who flourished in the Kivu provinces before the outbreak of the war.[14]

A legacy of the Congo War that is related to these two trends is the disruption caused by conflict to subsistence agriculture. Subsistence agriculture—a major part of direct entitlements—is not always disrupted by civil wars, but it has been severely affected in the DRC case. The war resulted in the ruination of some subsistence crops as cultivators, fearing marauders, fled their land. Some rebel groups also prevented villagers from cultivating fields and gathering food and wood in the forest, or limited the times when they could do so in an attempt to impede collaboration between them and other rebel groups.[15] Women in particular have refused to tend their fields out of fear of rape and other kinds of attacks by soldiers.[16] These fears have been deliberately encouraged by military actors—and validated by the sexual violence exacted upon women and girls by soldiers. The conflict has consequently reduced goods and services that were produced and consumed on a shared basis by the same household or extended family without a process of exchange. Since women made up a disproportionate size of the work force in the subsistence sector, their absence from the fields has had a negative impact on food production and has increased food shortages in rebel zones, as well as in government-controlled areas along the Congo River that were dependent on food from upstream sources in rebel-held eastern and northern DRC.

The exodus of labor from agriculture to mining has also had a deleterious effect on subsistence agriculture and overall food security, as fewer people have been available to produce food. In the Kivus and Oriental province, there has been a massive exodus of people from non-mining to mining areas as all age groups have tried to make a livelihood in the minerals sector. Along with the diversion of foodstuffs to mining enclaves—where more people have cash—political uncertainty has also eroded food security by causing higher food prices.

One effect of declining food security has been changing livestock practices. For example, in eastern DRC, some smallholders have shifted from the traditional practice of goat rearing to raising guinea pigs.[17] Goat rearing is inefficient in a context of insecurity, because goats cannot be carried when fighting erupts. Guinea pigs on the other hand are more portable, allowing owners to flee with their productive assets rather than leave them behind. This strategy has protected some smallholders from losing all of their livelihood.

The Congo War has also caused the erosion of direct entitlements through the negative impact on the environment caused by untrammeled exploitation of natural resources. Because much resource extraction has occurred illegally and the risk of losing control of an area has been high, loggers and miners have often worked to extract as many resources as quickly as possible and have had few incentives to conduct their operations in a manner that minimizes environmental damage. In the Kivus, for example, unregulated mining of coltan deposits underlying arable land has destabilized hillsides causing landslides that have destroyed fields. An estimated half of the land that has been seized for unplanned artisanal coltan mining is no longer suitable for agriculture.[18] In Ituri, coltan deposits lie in tropical forests, especially in national parks where miners hunt protected wildlife for food. Because coltan is slightly radioactive, streams now also contain radioactive residue (although the impact of this on both the environment and people remains unclear).[19] Destructive logging practices have been carried out "without considera- tion of any of the minimum acceptable rules of timber harvesting for sustainable forest management,"[20] and have produced soil erosion that has destroyed fisheries and wildlife habitat.

Table 5.1 illustrates the effect of the war on direct entitlements in the form of the production of subsistence crops. Laurent Kabila became president in May 1997 after a seven-month war that toppled Mobutu. A year later, most food crops, except sweet potatoes, experienced an increase of at least 1 percent. Clearly the effects of the anti-Kabila war were devastating for food production, which declined from 1999 to 2001—the worst case being that of the sweet potato, which declined almost 42 percent. Livestock production also declined after a brief increase in 1998.

In addition to direct entitlements, the Congo War has also had a neg- ative affect on market entitlements, including people's assets, what they gain from their labor, and the prices they pay to get essentials such as food and other services. Many belligerents have forced cultivators to sell

Table 5.1 Entitlements and Changing Agricultural Production

	1997	1998	1999	2000	2001
Direct entitlements (subsistence sector; production in thousands of metric tons)					
Beans	135	138	130	122	114
Cassava	16,973	17,060	16,500	15,969	15,436
Maize	1,167	1,215	1,199	1,184	1,169
Millet	52	54	33	34	35
Rice, paddy	355	363	350	338	326
Sweet potatoes	404	390	300	237	228
Market entitlements (produced for sale; 1997 = 100)					
Livestock	100.0	100.5	98.1	97.4	96.9
Food production	100.0	101.9	98.7	96.0	93.0
Cash crops	100.0	101.4	97.7	94.7	92.3

Source: Food and Agriculture Organization, *Production Yearbook* (Rome: FAO Publications, 2002).

their crops at depressed prices and have coerced local miners into relinquishing a portion of their finds to armed groups. As land and trading routes came under the control of armed groups, civilian economic opportunities were further constrained. At military checkpoints, sometimes set up solely for the purpose of collecting revenue, passengers have been required to dismount, wait in lengthy queues, display their packages, and pay bribes—all increasing the cost of bringing goods to market. Even in the wake of the peace accord, hostility and insecurity continue to constrain travel and thus commerce. For example, it is much easier to fly from the eastern town of Goma to Kinshasa 1,250 kilometers away than to travel by road from Goma to Butembo only 235 kilometers away. This is because the two towns are controlled by different political groups—although both are part of the transitional government—that limit travel between the two.[21] The net result of such constraints is a real decline in market exchanges that lower farmers' market entitlements.

The Congo War has also caused a reconfiguration of property rights, particularly land ownership, which has disrupted food production and reduced direct and market entitlements. Control over instruments of violence, rather than customary or legal title, became the deciding factor in determining land ownership and use. Against the wishes of rightful owners, land has been forcibly occupied, claimed, and exploited for minerals, rather than used for agriculture or for livestock production. The reconfiguration of land tenure has fed communal tensions and exacerbated ethnic divisions. For example, changes in land tenure in eastern DRC has benefited Congolese of Hema and Tutsi descent, who have been generally supported by the Ugandan and Rwandan forces that have gained control of lands that did not previously belong to them.

Unfortunately, customary methods to resolve disputes over land tenure have also been severely undermined during the Congo War as a result of customary authorities being unable to compete with, or control, combatants. As discussed in Chapter 2, there is an ongoing history of land disputes in eastern DRC. The first deadly clash over land since the 1960s occurred between Banyarwanda and other groups in North Kivu in 1993, resulting in the deaths of more than 12,000 people.[22] By early 1994, customary chiefs were able to stop the violence, settle the land issue without Kinshasa's interference, and bring some semblance of peace in the area.[23] The arrival of refugees in mid-1994 following the Rwandan genocide comprehensively destroyed this local solution. In the section "Toward Sustainable Peace," I analyze the issue of customary authority in more detail and argue for its restoration.

It comes as no surprise that customary authorities have been undermined, because civil war in general creates alternative institutional structures based on the use of violence to accumulate wealth and sustain political power, such as militia organizations, parallel market networks, and ethnic-based organizations.[24] Yet the current institutional environment of the DRC is not solely a product of the Congo War. Institutional legacies of the ancien régime—including the kinds of decisionmaking patterns related to land, ethnicity, and citizenship outlined in Chapter 2—remain salient. The reason such institutional legacies continue to influence the state is linked to what the conflict did *not* do: it did not deliver a complete military victory to one side.

Which institutions and which institutional legacies persist in a post-conflict environment is simpler when one party wins a civil war, such as occurred in Uganda in 1986, Ethiopia-Eritrea in 1991, and Rwanda in 1994. As the cases of Angola and Liberia indicate, the institutional legacies of the old regime tend to influence the transitional period after conflicts where there has been no clear-cut victory and where a transitional government, or government of national unity involving all sides involved in the conflict, is established.[25] Unfortunately, transitional governments are also more likely to fail than entirely new regimes, because negotiated settlements are more likely to break down than settlements based on military victories.[26]

In the DRC, dialogue and peace accords resulted in the creation of a transitional government, and it is this institution that must tackle the pernicious legacies of both the old regime and the power structures created during the Congo War, even while it is influenced by these legacies itself. Some transitional governments navigate these tensions well. For example, the transitional government of Mozambique was able to create a postconflict institutional setting that both bridged the structures of wartime and peace and created the structures needed to support peace, state building, and democracy.[27] The critical issue is the initial path chosen in the peace process, because it will establish institutional precedents that will structure the postconflict institutional framework. It is not yet clear what institutional path the transitional government has chosen for the DRC, but the lack of action by the government and the international community on several critical issues (as analyzed in the following section) suggests that neither the institutional legacies of the Mobutu era nor the Congo War will be effectively addressed.

Reconstruction

Reconstruction is critical for the future peace and prosperity of the DRC, and efforts to date have achieved some major successes.

Fortunately, considerable international assistance has been forthcoming, because without external assistance, economic, social, or political change would be very difficult to achieve.

Reconstruction efforts have been multipronged, involving the international community's sponsorship of economic programs (delivered by the IMF and World Bank) and DDRRR and disarmament, demobilization, and reintegration (DDR) programs (by the MONUC and the UNDP respectively—DDR excludes repatriation and resettlement as it focuses on Congolese nationals rather than on foreign combatants). Organizations such as the World Health Organization (WHO), the United Nations Children's Fund (UNICEF), and foreign NGOs are also funding programs to strengthen infrastructure for health and education services; the international community is aware that failure to expand access to basic health care and education may create widespread frustration and lower the chances for sustained postwar reconstruction. There are also new regulatory arrangements designed to promote economic growth.

Overall, reconstruction efforts have delivered benefits. However, benefits are yet to reach most of the population, the economic programs of international financial institutions (IFIs) do not necessarily complement efforts to strengthen social services, and there is tension between the differing reconstruction priorities of international agencies. Furthermore, reconstruction programs have tended to focus on the causes of current instability rather than on the causes of the conflict itself.

Economic Programs

A major component of the international community's reconstruction efforts is the economic programs being delivered by IFIs. Contemporary, liberal, macroeconomic policy of IFIs distinguishes between short-run stabilization and medium-to-long-run adjustment programs. *Adjustment*, which is the domain of the World Bank and regional development banks, refers to policies designed to alter economic structures; *stabilization* primarily involves fiscal and monetary policy supervised by the IMF. Additional policy initiatives for economic recovery and sustainable development in conflict or postconflict situations have also been developed by the IMF and World Bank with the aim of restoring effective and equitable governance of natural resources.

As of January 2005, the World Bank had approved a total of eighty-six loans and credits worth approximately U.S.$3.62 billion to revitalize the following sectors: agriculture, fishing, forestry, education, health, social services, transportation, law and public administration, energy, mining, water, finance, information, and communications.[28] In 2002, the Bank provided approximately $1.7 billion in cofinancing through its Emergency Multi-sector Rehabilitation and Reconstruction Project to support investment in infrastructure and sectoral reform.[29] In 2003, it approved a $120 million loan for a Private Sector Development and Competitiveness Project, a $214 million loan for a Post-Reunification Economic Recovery Project (PRERP) with the same goals of supporting ongoing sectoral and structural reforms, and a $178 million support package—via a Southern African Market Program—to upgrade the DRC's power grid to enable it to export electricity to southern Africa. In 2004, it approved an additional credit of $200 million to support the PRERP for reform of the civil service, and a grant of $102 million for a program to slow the spread of HIV/AIDS and to improve the lives of people living with AIDS. The latter uses local communities to help identify priorities and implement projects and is one of the few reconstruction projects to do so. A further $60 million has been provided to improve access by the poor to social and health services, to build community capacity to provide such services, and to provide educational scholarships and basic literacy programs.

In keeping with its institutional objectives, the IMF has focused more broadly on the DRC's macroeconomic performance. In 2001, IMF staff and the DRC government agreed on the implementation of a Staff-Monitored Program (SMP) from June 2001 to March 2002 to correct macroeconomic "disequilibria" by stabilizing the economy and laying the foundation for economic growth and reconstruction.[30] The goal of the SMP is to give the DRC government the opportunity to establish a strong track record in macroeconomic management that could lead to the clearance of arrears with the IMF, which would then deliver a more extensive program of assistance under its Poverty Reduction and Growth Facility (PRGF). The DRC government is required to implement the IMF's usual restrictive monetary and fiscal policies as well as other market-related policies, such as a floating exchange rate. It is also required to introduce economic liberalization policies. For example, its diamond monopoly was abolished in February 2001, and price controls were removed from all commodities with the exception of transportation, water, and electricity (which had controlled increases of 167 percent, 663 percent, and 270 percent, respectively). The SMP was updated following the July 2003 peace accords to take into account the ongoing implementation of the DDRRR program, the impact of the country's reunification, and the mobilization of external donor assistance.[31]

An assessment of the SMP by IMF staff in early 2002 indicated that the DRC authorities had steadfastly implemented the SMP and "brought about a courageous shifting of economic policy after years of mismanagement, corruption, and civil strife."[32] Seeking additional funds to build on these encouraging macroeconomic results, the DRC government requested a three-year PRGF, from April 2002 to July 2005. The IMF approved a loan of $580 million in special drawing rights under the PRGF to this end, the goals being to achieve real growth of 5 percent per year, to reduce the annual inflation rate to 6 percent, and to increase foreign currency reserves.

Economic indicators have, indeed, improved. Inflation dropped from 511 percent in 2000 to 15 percent in 2002, and growth in real GDP improved from -7 percent in 2000 to 3 percent in 2002 and reached 5 percent in 2003 (a thirteen-year high). The IMF further estimated that real GDP would increase by 4 percent in 2004 and by 7 percent in 2005.[33] One consequence of this remarkable turnaround has been the stabilization of the exchange rate under a floating exchange system. The disparity between the official and parallel exchange rate narrowed from 600 percent before the floating rate system to 1 percent at the end of December 2001. The IMF and the DRC government are also working together to expand the banking sector as an intermediary between the central bank and the public, by encouraging banking transactions (or intermediation) and discouraging "dollarization" (the use of dollars) in domestic transactions. Because of the current low levels of intermediation, the ability of the central bank to carry out its major monetary policies is constrained. However, expanding intermediation is a challenging task in the DRC, where people have never trusted the banking system and have always preferred to keep their savings in pillows, mattresses, and jars.

An area of continuing macroeconomic concern is government spending, which the IMF projects will keep increasing (from 8.2 percent of GDP in 2001 to 21.5 percent of GDP by 2006), while revenue will increase from 6.5 percent of GDP to 11 percent.[34] Naturally, the government must either borrow or print more money to finance the difference between revenue and expenditure. Nevertheless, investors have been encouraged by the overall economic picture, and the government has approved more than 100 investment applications from the domestic and international private sector, amounting to $2.3 billion for the period 2003–2007.[35]

The rosy macroeconomic picture reported by IMF staff belies some underlying problems. The IMF reports that the successful implementation of its DRC program has eliminated "smuggling to neighboring countries" and has "increased the supply of basic foodstuffs from the producing regions to the cities and lowered prices, although progress in this regard continued to be hampered by the lack of road maintenance."[36] These claims are exaggerated. First, Congo-Brazzaville, Rwanda, and especially Uganda continue to export diamonds even though these countries do not produce diamonds. In late 2004, one year after signing the Kimberley Process Certification Scheme (KPCS) to regulate international trade in diamonds, the Congo-Brazzaville government was accused of participating in an illegal diamond trade worth more than $100 million. It was subsequently expelled from the agreement.[37] Clearly, smuggling to these countries from the DRC continues to occur. Second, while the IMF has been able to control the parallel currency market in Kinshasa and Lower Congo, the rest of the country largely remains dollarized. In eastern DRC, dollars are the only means of payment, store of value, and instrument of deferred payment.[38] Third, although the situation at the macrolevel is improving, the situation at the microlevel is not. An economic survey of eastern DRC conducted by NGOs in 2004 indicates that household incomes have declined further as the informal sector that provided citizens with a means of survival has been detrimentally affected by conflict.[39] Fourth, while the IMF has proven its commitment to transparency and accountability in the extractive industry as part of its overall package of fiscal reform in the DRC, it misunderstands the role of enclave economies created by illegal mining of coltan and diamonds and consequently has ignored their importance. Mining enclaves are the source of much of the country's economic activity and foreign exchange, but the IMF has little information on the phenomenon of enclaves and their role in the broader economy.

The IMF also issued a general assessment that the transitional government is "functioning well."[40] This overlooks the fact that international pressure is the key factor keeping the government together, and the reports of scandals and corruption that abound in local press suggest the IMF's confidence may be misplaced. Joseph Kabila has appointed cronies from Katanga province to head state-owned enterprises, and former rebel members of the government have been demanding that jobs in state-owned companies be divided along the same political lines as in the power-sharing government. Although an anticorruption strategy has been introduced for the public sector, the critical issue in reducing corruption is ensuring that public officials receive a living wage. Yet public servants in Kinshasa—earning $50 per month—had not been paid for months. By contrast, the managers of state companies are receiving packages ranging from $15,000 to $25,000 a month.[41]

Finally, although economic discipline on the part of the DRC government—a priority of the IMF—is necessary if the government is to manage the economy in a manner that promotes long-term growth, applying economic discipline may conflict with the goal of political stability. When designing postconflict policies and seeking to establish an enduring peace, political stability cannot be relegated to a lower priority than economic efficiency. Reconstruction efforts may be nullified if war starts anew, and the restoration of confidence among legitimate foreign and national investors largely depends on it.

There is also a general problem with the uniformity of the IMF's policies across time and space. Although such uniformity provides the IMF with a yardstick by which to evaluate policy performance, it ignores variations from one country to another. Operationally, the IMF's DRC program is typical of its one-size-fits-all approach, designed to bridge the gap between aggregate demand and aggregate supply and to create favorable conditions for market operations. The advantage of such an approach is that it eliminates the controls and regulations that have blocked the functioning of market mechanisms, such as those instituted by both rebel groups and the central government on investments, production, prices, wages, imports, and exports. Indeed, a system of liberalization is critical if rent-seeking activities and illegal exploitation of natural resources are to be minimized. Yet the IMF's programs for the DRC and other countries have remained largely the same whether applied during peacetime or during postconflict periods. The utility of policies that have not worked in times of peace—IMF imposed more than fourteen stabilization programs on the Mobutu government between 1976 to 1991 without any long-term positive effects[42]—is even more doubtful in postconflict situations.

In contrast to the macrolevel policies of the IMF, the World Bank has targeted the microlevel in order to improve conditions for local communities, and this focus is commendable. But its program is experiencing implementation difficulties. Eastern DRC, which has suffered more than any other region of the country, remains under the military control of different militias and is politically unstable, and across the DRC the Bank's programs lack the input required from local communities that is essential for its programs to work. Most significantly, neither the World Bank's nor the IMF's programs of postwar reconstruction address some of the root causes of the conflict: citizenship and land issues and the manipulation of these issues by Congolese politicians.

DDRRR and DDR

The demilitarization of foreign and Congolese former combatants remains a daunting task and is being addressed through a process of disarmament, demobilization, and reintegration that has become "a standard tool of UN missions and donors in countries emerging from armed conflict."[43] Three organizations are in charge of the process. The MONUC is mandated to deal with the DDRRR of foreign combatants still in the DRC, and the UNDP focuses on the disarmament, demobilization, and reintegration (DDR) of Congolese forces—a program that is linked to the World Bank-funded Multi-Country Demobilization and Reintegration Program (MDRP).[44] The World Bank is a key player in delivering assistance programs to the DRC and ensuring that delivery is synchronized for maximum effectiveness. The MDRP program provides financial and technical assistance to national programs, regional initiatives, and special projects that fit the criteria of the World Bank's African Great Lakes regional strategy for demobilization and reintegration.

The MONUC's DDRRR program officially began on February 22, 2001, after the UN Security Council passed Resolution 1341, which authorized the deployment of 550 UN military observers to the DRC and set a timetable for the signatories of the Lusaka peace agreement to withdraw their military forces. In practice, it was not until the second half of 2002 that implementation actually began in several towns, and this was only on an ad hoc basis pending deployment of the two task forces to be based in Kindu and Kisangani, as recommended by UN Security Council Resolution S/2002/1005. The MONUC's DDRRR program is based on Chapter 9 of the Lusaka peace agreement, which stipulates that the disarmament of warring parties should be voluntary and be undertaken at the initiative of the signatories themselves.[45] In the spirit of this accord, MONUC established a Joint Coordination Committee for DDRRR and has continued consulting with the World Bank to refine their division of labor and to transform the DDRRR concept into a joint operational plan.

The design of the MONUC's DRC mission has several flaws, principally related to its role in disarming foreign combatants. As a result of the Lusaka accords, MONUC has a mandate to identify, screen, demobilize, and repatriate combatants, but it has no role in their *disarmament*. Implementation of DDRRR has therefore been inconsistent because it depends on disarmament—which has either not occurred or been incomplete, situations that have delayed planned subsequent repatriation, resettlement, and reintegration. In some instances, the MONUC's activities have even reinforced local power imbalances as one group of combatants has been voluntarily disarmed but others have not. Because the Lusaka accords have not addressed the vested economic interests of warring parties, the MONUC has also been unable to address the issue of economic interests. Yet these interests are linked to the willingness of combatants to disarm.

In DDRRR programs in other postconflict situations, two strategies have usually been employed as incentives for belligerents to voluntarily disarm: programs that trade food or agricultural implements for weapons, and cash "buy-backs" of weapons—the former being more successful than the latter. To be successful, these programs require the setting of clear deadlines (after which any possession of weapons is punishable), immediately followed by resettlement and reintegration of former combatants by providing them viable alternative livelihoods.[46] The latter must be in keeping with the economy of the communities into which former combatants will be integrated, although they may demand slightly better economic opportunities—after all, they need incentives to disarm and reintegrate. The Ethiopian case is instructive in this regard. After the fall of the Mengistu regime in 1991, former combatants who returned to uplands crop farming received coffee plants, those returning to lowland wheat cultivation received draft animals, and those returning to urban areas received apprenticeships, small business management, and microcredit.[47] Unfortunately, clear deadlines and incentives sensitive to conditions in the DRC are lacking in the MONUC's DDRRR program—as they are also lacking in the Lusaka accords.

The MONUC's efforts have been undermined in some localities because of specific events on the ground. For example, in early 2003, progovernment armed militia members had assembled in eastern DRC to enter the MONUC's DDRRR program when they were attacked by RCD-Goma forces. The militia members dispersed into the forest, making it very difficult for MONUC to reestablish contact with them. By January 2005, the MONUC had repatriated less than 20 percent of foreign combatants (11,300 people—mostly to Rwanda, Burundi, and Uganda), leaving an estimated 54,000 still scattered throughout the DRC.[48] These numbers included 8,000 to 10,000 combatants of the exiled FDLR, who launch attacks on Rwanda out of their bases in DRC territory and target Kinyarwanda-speaking Congolese communities. The FDLR pose one of the most serious threats to peace, because they both cause the Rwandan military to maintain close links with RCD militias in the DRC and tempt it to reenter the DRC in pursuit.[49]

The MONUC has also not been able to successfully implement the UN

Security Council's Resolution 1492 (2003), which sought to complement disarmament efforts by introducing an embargo on the importation of arms into Ituri, North Kivu, and South Kivu and giving the organization the authority to seize weaponry within the DRC. Key problems have been the MONUC's inability to "verify information concerning violations of the embargo because of its limited presence and denial of access," and the international community's lack of progress in establishing an arms monitoring mechanism.[50] Moreover, the mission's ability to monitor a 2,500-kilometer border, including 1,000 kilometers with Burundi, Rwanda, and Uganda, is hampered by rain forest, a myriad of small airstrips, and smuggling tracks. There has also been a total lack of cooperation on Resolution 1492 by neighboring governments, especially Rwanda.

The initial phase of the UNDP's DDR program focusing on Congolese former combatants targeted vulnerable groups, such as child soldiers, the war-injured and disabled, chronically ill soldiers, widows, and orphans. The second phase focused on the unification and restructuring of forces as set out in the Lusaka accords. These multilateral efforts have been augmented by the actions of the DRC authorities, Joseph Kabila having issued presidential decree-law 066 of June 6, 2000, which authorized the demobilization and reintegration of vulnerable soldier groups. Implementation of the decree-law was bestowed on the Departments of Defense and Human Rights, as well as the Bureau National de Démobilisation et de Réintégration, which the DRC government created to work with the World Bank, ILO, and UNICEF.

The UNDP's DDR program has a more realistic scope than the MONUC's DDRRR program, but it has suffered from delays and confusion about which organizations are actually responsible for what tasks. In the third quarter of 2001, the UNDP was nominated as the lead agency for the DDR of Congolese combatants, but it was only endorsed as the lead agency one and a half years later, in February 2003, when it became officially responsible for 320,000 ex-combatants, including former members of the FAC, RCD-Goma, MLC, RCD-ML, and Mai Mai militias. But by this time, the World Bank had already begun implementing its regional approach to DDRRR involving nine countries, including the DRC.

Like the DDRRR of foreign combatants, the DDR of Congolese former combatants is also an ongoing problem, with 200,000 yet to be demobilized. A key problem is that demobilization programs are compromised by disagreements and misunderstandings regarding the eligibility criteria of combatants to receive assistance through the UNDP's program. The IMF remarked with regard to this issue that "no clarity existed by the end of 2003 from the government or the armed groups, and it became increasingly difficult to manage the expectations of the large numbers of potential beneficiaries."[51] It was not until late 2003 that President Joseph Kabila promulgated several decrees establishing an interministerial DDR committee (the National Disarmament, Demobilization, and Reintegration Commission) to facilitate DDR, and it was only in 2004 that the Security Council finally approved the use of force by MONUC troops to demobilize recalcitrant rebel militias. In early 2004, the transitional government, assisted by the UNDP, started a program of disarmament and reintegration into the community for an estimated 15,000 eligible militia members in the Ituri region. By mid-December 2004, only 1,056 former combatants including 424 male and 69 female children had even registered for the program.[52]

Finally, donors have ignored the role and opinions of local communities in the DDR program and have assumed that ex-combatants would be accepted by their former neighbors without investigating whether this was the case. The end of any civil war does not mean that people will easily accept to live or work beside those who killed their children, parents, and grandparents or who raped their wives and children. Because many former combatants have participated in such crimes, they may be rejected by their communities or subject to revenge. Communities need to be educated as to the benefits of accepting former combatants and probably also need to be offered some incentives. In turn, former combatants must earn the trust of the community. Clearly donors should not take for granted that former combatants will be accepted without opposition.

Not all troops are to be completely demobilized. Approximately 120,000 former combatants are to be integrated into a new national army, the Forces Armées de la République Démocratique du Congo (FARDC). Regional commanders have been appointed to the FARDC, but there has been little progress toward creating an integrated national army. A key problem is that different organizations have been established to deal with combatants, resulting in problems of coordination, particularly in obtaining the simultaneous disarmament needed to build confidence that neither side is gaining a military advantage from the process.[53] Former rebel members of the transitional government have also failed to fulfill their pledge to integrate militia leaders into the FARDC.

New Regulatory Frameworks

Challenges created by the war economy for the natural resources sector have highlighted the overall need for improved regulation and management of that sector in the DRC, in terms of both the government's management of revenue and expenditure and the social impact of exploitation. New regulatory frameworks have long been sought by the formal mining industry (including both Congolese and foreign players), but it is only in the current policy environment of reconstruction that such frameworks have been able to be introduced. More generally, the importance of natural resources in perpetuating contemporary conflicts around the world has also made the regulation of resource flows a priority for policymakers involved in conflict prevention and management.[54] These twin pressures for reform have seen the introduction of new domestic and international regulatory frameworks that are shaping the way Congolese resources are produced and marketed.

In 2002, following a determination that revitalization of the natural resources sector was essential for reconstruction, the DRC government, with assistance from the World Bank, finally introduced its new code of investment for the mining industry in conjunction with a National Investment Promotion Agency that is designed to be a *guichet unique* (one-stop window) for processing investment applications and information. In line with international practices, the code provides "a level playing field through transparent incentives for domestic and foreign investors alike and clarifies the rights and responsibilities of investors, regulatory agencies, regional governments, and the fiscal authorities."[55] The new code serves the formal mining sector well in that it has created a stable and favorable regulatory environment. However, it has created uncertainty for the artisanal sector. Under Article 26 of the code, only adult individuals with Congolese citizenship may obtain an artisanal miner's card, but there is no clear law on citizenship. This makes the new system open to discrimination, corruption, and inefficiency. Moreover, children do not qualify for a card, despite the fact that they represent a substantial proportion of the mining labor force, especially on mines controlled by warlords in eastern DRC. In any case, bureaucracy and corruption are likely to delay the distribution of miners' cards across all the far-flung artisanal sites in the DRC.

The KPCS aims to establish minimum common rules for rough diamond certification and is the first certification system of its kind to try to regulate the trade in conflict goods.[56] It is one of several regulatory frameworks to have been introduced in recent years to combat specific global "ills," including money laundering, narcotics trafficking, international organized crime, terrorism, and violent conflicts involving natural resources.[57] The KPCS relies on a certification of origin and a chain of warranties to provide an audit trail that links diamonds to their mine of origin, thus preventing diamonds illicitly produced in conflict areas from reaching international markets and also reducing their profitability to criminals and combatants. Its purpose is to reduce the violent and illegal exploitation of diamonds during civil wars.[58] Unfortunately, the process penalizes artisanal miners who do not use violent methods and who have established some kind of land-use right but who happen to live in a country experiencing a civil conflict. In countries such as the DRC, the artisanal sector for all minerals occurs in legal "gray" zones—even during times of peace. Furthermore, as for informal economies in general, the artisanal diamond sector can provide benefits for civilian populations.[59] Diamond production in countries experiencing conflict must therefore be carefully assessed so that any policy or regulatory strategy distinguishes the criminal activities of armed groups from the informal survival strategies of local mining communities, and does not have an unduly harsh impact on the latter.

One model of managing revenue from natural resources that has received much analytical attention is the Chad-Cameroon Petroleum Development and Pipeline Project (CCP), which involves the World Bank Group, three transnational oil companies (ExxonMobil, Chevron, and Petronas Malaysia), and the governments of Chad and Cameroon. The CCP has the broad goals of exploiting Chad's oil resources in a socially responsible manner and distributing revenue in a way that benefits all major stakeholders, including the Chadian and Cameroonian public, by ensuring that oil revenues are used to improve the lives of affected communities and populations.[60] A key aim is to minimize the kinds of corruption that have plagued resource developments in other oil-rich countries, such as Angola.

There are three major weaknesses with the project's design, and each contains a useful lesson for any similar project that might be introduced to the DRC. First, revenue management policies will not achieve their intended effect unless there is an accountable and transparent government. This probably means a government answerable to the public. The government of Chad does not meet this criteria and nor does the DRC government. Furthermore, it is not clear that the international monitoring bodies designed to have oversight of the project can actually pressure host governments to improve fiscal and social accountability. Second, the World Bank's independent inspection panel has criticized the project for allocating only 5 percent of royalties from oil revenues to the producing region in Chad, and for inadequately ensuring that these profits would be distributed as agreed under the management plan. This bodes ill for any similar model to be used for the DRC, where regional tensions over the distribution of resource revenues are already acute. Third, given the level of revenue returned to the producing region, this kind of partnership will work only if the transnational corporation itself, rather than the government, is required to build infrastructure such as schools and hospitals that can be used by company workers and surrounding communities. Yet this risks replicating and recreating the dominance of mining companies, such as that of Gécamines in the DRC for most of the twentieth century. Despite these problems, it may be possible to adapt a version of the CCP to the DRC if single, more capable, and transparent institutions are selected and if there is fairness in, and rigorous adherence to, revenue sharing.

Toward Sustainable Peace

Multilateral reconstruction programs and associated programs of the DRC government fail to address several specific issues that are essential to long-term economic, political, and social stability. What these issues have in common is their relevance to the grassroots communities that form the bulk of the Congolese population and their relationship to the economic dimensions of the conflict—either because they are a consequence of the conflict, or a cause. This section details issues that are not addressed by current reconstruction efforts but that must be if a lasting peace is to be successfully established.

First and foremost are disputes over property rights. The conflict resulted in houses, land, and other property being seized by militias (and in some cases by the communities that support them), or simply occupied as their original owners fled conflict. Unless the transitional government and the international community undertake a concerted effort to restore previous property rights, conflicts will resurface during the postreconstruction phase as former owners return home to claim their ownership rights. Restitution of land, in particular, will be difficult as ownership and use of land have become confused by the granting of concessions by different authorities (such as by both the DRC government and rebel groups), as well as by actors occupying the land using force.

The formal mining sector has been affected by uncertainty resulting from confusion over property rights. The sector is a major source of foreign currency for the DRC and the key attraction for foreign investors. There is therefore an urgent need to clarify mining companies' claims to existing concessions. This issue is being addressed by a review of wartime contracts, but the review was not born out of the government's desire to allay the fears of mining companies. Rather, it originated as an agenda item of the ICD in response to the first report of the UN Panel of Experts that exposed the exploitation of resources by Rwandan and Ugandan forces. As ever, this task is more complicated in eastern DRC, which has been under the rule of competing authorities and where unauthorized mining by companies linked to members of the transitional government has taken place over the past seven years. Nevertheless, the transitional government established a committee that has reviewed mining contracts granted by both rebel groups and the government during the conflict. Where more than one contract exists, the committee will determine which contract has the greatest validity. The problem is that the criteria for validating concessions are unclear, opening the possibility for corruption in the validation process.

The whole issue of legality versus illegality is complicated with regard to property rights and user rights (such as mining concessions). Although the conceptual definition of *legal* is unambiguous—permitted by the law—its operational definition depends on those who control the reins of government. Because the actors that have been illegally exploiting natural resources in eastern DRC are now partners in the transitional government, does this mean that formally illicit exploitation has been legalized? More significantly, agents of the DRC state have also participated in the violent and criminal exploitation of diamonds, such as the seizure of Miba's concessions and the use by government elites of armed men to expel artisanal miners from mine sites (see Chapter 3). It would seem that as long as contracts were signed in the capital city, they have acquired legality regardless of the person who signs the contract.

Such a situation is detrimental to the artisanal mining sector, which remains at the mercy of powerful players and mining companies. Artisanal diamond, gold, and coltan miners and their families probably number in the millions, and their economic and social importance—as well as, one could speculate, their political importance in any future election—has been neglected by reconstruction efforts and hindered by the DRC government's own policies. The government's new mining code has contributed to this situation through its restrictive provisions regarding artisanal mining.

The issues outlined in this section cannot be addressed by current multinational organizations' reconstruction programs because they are not designed to tackle such issues. Unfortunately, the transitional government is also not well equipped to address these issues, partly because it is compromised by a membership that clearly has economic interests of its own that overlap with artisanal miners, mining companies, and communities seeking restitution of lands. By contrast, customary authorities may be able to play such a role. While some customary authorities have been compromised in the eyes of communities by their links to the Mobutu regime and criminal economic activities during the Congo War, other customary authorities continue to play an important role in maintaining social stability and in resolving local conflicts. They also understand their communities better than rebels turned vice presidents and ministers. Indeed, despite their usurpation by armed groups, customary authorities retain considerable legitimacy among much of the population—even if they remain militarily weak—and must be involved in postconflict efforts if the state is to be effective and responsive to community needs. In particular, the DDR process in the countryside can be made more effective with the consent and help of customary authorities. For example, the integration of former combatants into their villages may require the allocation of plots of land to the combatants and their families if reintegration is to be successful. Customary chiefs may be the only people with the authority to grant land for this purpose.

Customary authorities could also be used to settle disputes over property rights. This is especially the case in eastern DRC where systems of tribute based on Bwami associations[61] have remained intact, even in South Kivu through the gold rush and confusion over property rights that occurred in that province in the 1980s. Efforts to clarify competing rights to former agricultural land that has been turned into coltan or diamond mining sites could usefully draw upon customary law, which has been used historically by customary authorities to settle disputes. Customary law defines the use of land in terms of communal rights that separate *ownership* from *use*. This separation of rights could, with suitable compensation, potentially satisfy both miners and customary landowners. Using customary law, however, would require the transitional government to recognize customary authorities as a political institution with a formal role in governance.

Conclusion

Reconstruction efforts in the DRC have produced successes in terms of improving the macroeconomic climate and creating a more stable institutional environment. However, these efforts risk failure because they inadequately address economic interests that have been created and sustained by the conflict and that continue to create tensions. In particular, the macroeconomic stabilization programs and conventional structural adjustment strategies that are being crafted and imposed by donors and the international community need to be adapted to the specific challenges of the DRC's conflict/postconflict setting—as is the case for other countries in which such programs are implemented.

A key weakness of reconstruction efforts in general is that they risk duplicating the mistakes of postconflict reconstruction efforts elsewhere—namely, waste and replication—due to insufficient coordination between donors. The policies of the IMF, for example, tend to be implemented in isolation from both other donor agencies and peace missions and also ignore related vital issues, such as political stability and the restoration of basic infrastructure, that are so critical to sustain peace in postconflict periods.[62] Elizabeth Cousens has demonstrated that in the case of reconstruction efforts in Bosnia following that country's civil war, the considerable political and military resources of the international community were neither productively linked to one another nor harnessed to a well-conceived common strategy to build peace. The main problems were the absence of a clear delineation of responsibilities and the subsequent emergence of different—and sometimes divergent—strategies to implement the same types of program.[63] In the DRC case, the International Committee to Support the Transition (ICST)—composed of fifteen closely interested governments, including the five permanent Security Council members—has been given the task of coordinating assistance. However, the ICST is largely focused on security and is not sufficiently involved in coordinating the activities of individual donors.

Reconstruction efforts have also tended to marginalize local communities and regional organizations. Without participation by local communities in both planning and implementation, it will be difficult to create enduring solutions to the conflict. Most importantly, reconstruction strategies need to focus more on the microlevel economic conditions of households, and in the current environment this means improving both conditions for subsistence production and food security. Informal activities in general—but especially artisanal mining—need to be better addressed by reconstruction efforts, notwithstanding the difficulties caused by their legal "grayness." Reconstruction programs must also ensure that economic programs benefit rather than penalize the communities involved in such activities. They also need to address outstanding issues, such as the tensions over property rights, that are at the core of political tensions manifested as ethnic and citizenship disputes. Cooperation on the part of donors and the transitional government with customary authorities could facilitate both analyses of these problems and help with their resolution.

Despite the importance of these economically related measures, the key focus of reconstruction efforts should be getting social policies right, strengthening state institutions, and moving away from a narrow focus on macroeconomic discipline. This emphasis is essential in conflicts that have involved widespread economic predation that has systematically altered civilian livelihoods and resulted in large proportions of a population becoming dependent on technically criminal economic activities. Therefore, while this chapter—and the book—have focused on the economic dimensions of the Congo War, social justice is also central to achieving successful postwar reconciliation and reconstruction.

It is critical that war victims obtain some form of justice for crimes committed against them, including compensation for destruction of livelihoods, because a lasting peace is unlikely unless citizens feel that past crimes are appropriately dealt with and will not be repeated or tolerated in the future. The transitional government has barely addressed these issues, probably because those in the government, especially former rebels, were the ones responsible for many of the atrocities that occurred. The transitional government must, however, formally acknowledge that abuses occurred and create a reconciliation commission to document the nature and extent of human rights violations committed during the war. Ideally, such a commission would also have some powers to prosecute the worst and most senior offenders. But social justice cannot be achieved without addressing those tough perennial issues of DRC politics: citizenship and land. Unless these are made central to the reconstruction efforts of both the international community and the transitional government, those efforts risk failure.

Notes

1. For example, in early 2005, the European Union suspended two projects in Nyabondo, North Kivu province, that were intended to rehabilitate the road between Masisi and Walikale but suffered systematic looting of installations of the NGO German Agro Action by militiamen. The NGO lost 250 canisters of gasoline, 12,000 hoes that had been earmarked for farmers, 700 bags of cement, 600 metal sheets for schools and health centers, and engines (see *Integrated Regional Information Networks*, "DRC: EU Suspends Projects in North Kivu," March 2, 2005). In another example, in October 2004, a militia calling itself the Revolutionary Movement for the Liberation of Congo (RMLC) took control of Kilwa, a government-controlled town in eastern Katanga province, 50 kilometers from the Dikulushi copper-silver mine of the Australian company Anvil Mining. The militia claimed it wanted control of Dikulushi in

order to more fairly distribute mineral revenues—an unlikely scenario (Oxford Analytica, "Congo-Kinshasa: Resource Sector Brings Political Risks," Daily Briefing, July 20, 2005).

2. World Bank, *Transitional Support Strategy for the Democratic Republic of the Congo* (Washington, D.C.: International Development Association, January 2004), p. 9.

3. Bernadin Akitoby and Matthias Cinyabuguma, "Sources of Growth in the Democratic Republic of the Congo: An Econometric Approach," in Jean A. P. Clément, ed., *Postconflict Economics in Sub-Saharan Africa: Lessons from the Democratic Republic of the Congo* (Washington, D.C.: International Monetary Fund, 2004), p. 201.

4. International Crisis Group, *Pulling Back from the Brink in the Congo* (Nairobi: ICG, July 7, 2004), p. 2.

5. George Downs and Stephen. J. Stedman, "Evaluation Issues in Peace Implementation," in Stephen. J. Stedman, Donald Rothchild, and Elizabeth M. Cousens, eds., *Ending Civil Wars: The Implementation of Peace Agreements* (Boulder, Colo.: Lynne Rienner, 2002), pp. 55–56.

6. Ibid.

7. Amartya K. Sen, *Poverty and Famines* (Clarendon Press, 1981), pp. 1–7.

8. Jean Drèze and Amartya Sen, "Introduction," in Jean Drèze, Amartya Sen, and Athar Husain, eds., *The Political Economy of Hunger* (Oxford: Clarendon Press, 1995), p. 15.

9. S. O. Osmani, "The Food Problem of Bangladesh," in Drèze, Sen, and Husain, *The Political Economy of Hunger,* pp. 340–341.

10. Calculated from the DRC Banque Centrale's *Rapport Annuel* (Kinshasa: Banque Centrale, 2002), p. 76.

11. Ibid., p. 76.

12. See Aloys Tegera, Sofia Mikolo, and Dominic Johnson, *The Coltan Phenomenon* (Goma, DRC: Pole Institute, January 2002).

13. Ibid.

14. Kisangani F. Emizet, "Conflict in the Democratic Republic of Congo: A Mosaic of Insurgent Groups," *International Journal on World Peace* 20, no. 3 (September 2003): 70.

15. Human Rights Watch, *Eastern Congo Ravaged* (New York: Human Rights Watch, 2001), p. 17.

16. Joanne Cosete, *The War Within the War: Sexual Violence Against Women and Girls in Eastern Congo* (New York: Human Rights Watch, 2002), p. 49.

17. Pole Institute, *Natural Resource Exploitation and Human Security in the Democratic Republic of Congo,* Seminar Report (London and Goma, DRC: Pole Institute, February 2004), p. 8.

18. Tegera, Mikolo, and Johnson, "The Coltan Phenomenon," p. 20.

19. "Coltan," *African Research Bulletin,* July 16–August 15, 2004, p. 16204.

20. United Nations, *Report of the Panel of Experts on the Illegal Exploitation of Natural Resources and Other Forms of Wealth of the Democratic Republic of Congo* (New York: United Nations, 2001), paragraph 47.

21. Pole Institute, *Natural Resource Exploitation,* p. 7.

22. U.S. Committee for Refugees, *World Refugee Survey* (Washington, D.C.: Immigration and Refugee Services of America, 1994).

23. Ibid.

24. Mats Berdal and David Malone, eds., *Greed and Grievance: Economic Agendas in Civil Wars* (Boulder, Colo.: Lynne Rienner, 2000).

25. Nat J. Colletta, Markus Kostner, and Ingo Wiederhofer, *The Transition from War to Peace in Sub-Saharan Africa* (Washington, D.C.: U.S. Peace Institute, 1996).

26. See especially Robert H. Wagner, "The Causes of Peace," in Roy Licklider, ed., *Stopping the Killing* (New York: New York University Press, 1993); Roy Licklider, "The Consequences of Negotiated Settlements in Civil Wars, 1945–1993," *American Political Science Review* 89 (September 1995): 685.

27. Terrence Lyons, "Transforming the Institutions of War: Postconflict Elections and the Reconstruction of Failed States," in Robert I. Rotberg, ed., *When States Fail: Causes and Consequences* (Princeton: Princeton University Press, 2003), p. 271.

28. Figures were sourced from the country page for the DRC on the World Bank's website, http://web.worldbank.org, accessed March 20, 2005.

29. Clément, *Postconflict Economics*, p. 289, footnote 12.

30. International Monetary Fund, "DRC: 2001 Article IV Consultation and Discussions on Staff-Monitoring Program" (Washington, D.C: IMF Publication Services, July 2001), paragraph 13, p. 10.

31. International Monetary Fund, "DRC: Request for a Three-Year Arrangement Under the Poverty Reduction and Growth Facility and the First Annual Program—Staff Report" (Washington, D.C.: IMF, July 2002).

32. Jean A. P. Clément, "The Democratic Republic of the Congo: Lessons and Challenges for a Country Emerging from War," in Clément, *Postconflict Economics*, p. 24.

33. Ibid.

34. Ibid., p. 33.

35. Ibid., p. 38.

36. Ibid., p. 27.

37. "Republic of Congo, Expelled from World Diamond Trade for Alleged Smuggling, Signs Diamond Pact with Neighbors," *Associated Press Worldstream*, November 24, 2004.

38. A *means of payment* refers to the fact that people accept a currency such that people earning it at the present time can use it to buy goods and services from others. A currency functions as a *store of value* whenever people are willing to keep some of their wealth in the form of that currency, usually under the assumption that it is immune to inflationary or deflationary pressures. A currency is an instrument of *deferred payment* when people are willing to lend money to others knowing that when the money owed to them is repaid in the future, it will have the same purchasing power.

39. Pole Institute, *Natural Resource Exploitation*, pp. 7–9.

40. Clément, *Postconflict Economics*.

41. "Cruel By-Products of War," *Africa Research Bulletin,* June 16–July 15, 2004, p. 15936A.

42. Kisangani N. F. Emizet, *Zaire after Mobutu: A Case of a Humanitarian Emergency* (Helsinki: World Institute for Development Economics Research, 1997), p. 20.

43. David M. Malone and Heiko Nitzschke, "Economic Agendas in Civil Wars: What We Know, What We Need to Know," Discussion Paper No. 2005/07, April 2005, World Institute for Development Economics Research, p. 14.

44. The program was prepared in close collaboration with more than thirty multilateral and bilateral partners and governments of participating countries, which included Angola, Burundi, Central African Republic, DRC, Namibia, Congo, Rwanda, Uganda, and Zimbabwe.

45. In consultation with the government of Uganda, the MONUC has also embarked on a separate DDRRR program not included in the UNSC's initial resolution. The program involved the transportation of some 300 to 400 combatants of the Allied Democratic Front from eastern DRC to Uganda. The operation was expected to be conducted under the overall supervision of the Ugandan Amnesty Commission and the MONUC, in collaboration with other organizations. The Donor Technical Group on Uganda, which consisted of prominent international donors, agreed to finance the operation, in which the role of the MONUC was limited to disarming and demobilizing Allied Democratic Front combatants rather than coordinating the whole process.

46. Joanna Spear, "Disarmament and Demobilization," in Stedman, Rothchild, and Cousens, *Ending Civil Wars*, pp. 141–182; Nicole Ball, "Demobilizing and Reintegrating Soldiers," in Krishna Kumar, ed., *Rebuilding Societies After Civil War: Critical Roles for International Assistance* (Boulder, Colo.: Lynne Rienner, 1997), pp. 85–105.

47. United Nations Development Programme, *Harnessing Institutional Capacities in Support of the Disarmament, Demobilization, and Reintegration of Former Combatants*, paper prepared by the Executive Committee on Humanitarian Assistance Working Group on Disarmament, Demobilization, and Reintegration (New York: United Nations, 2000), pp. 1–40.

48. United Nations, *Sixteenth Report of the Secretary-General on the United Nations Organization Mission in the DRC*, S/2004/1034, December 31, 2004, p. 5.

49. International Crisis Group, *Back to the Brink in the Congo* (Nairobi: ICG, December 17, 2004).

50. United Nations, *Sixteenth Report*, p. 5.

51. Markus Kostner, Ely Dieng, and Andriaan Verhel, "The Long Road to Demilitarization," in Clément, *Postconflict Economics*, p. 321.

52. United Nations, *Sixteenth Report*, p. 3.

53. European Union, *Stratégie de Coopération et Programme Indicatif, République Démocratique du Congo, 2003–2007* (Brussels: European Union, 2003), p. 6.

54. Neil Cooper, "State Collapse as Business: The Role of Conflict Trade and the Emerging Control Agenda," *Development and Change* 33 (2002): 935–955; Ian Bannon and Paul Collier, eds., *Natural Resources and Violent Conflict: Options and Actions* (Washington, D.C.: World Bank, 2004).

55. Clément, *Postconflict Economics*, p. 286.

56. J. Andrew Grant and Ian Taylor, "Global Governance and Conflict Diamonds: The Kimberley Process and the Quest for Clean Gems," *The Round Table* 93 (2004): 10.

57. Malone and Nitzschke, "Economic Agendas in Civil Wars," p. 10.

58. See www.kimberleyprocess.com.

59. Musifiki Mwanasali, "The View from Below," in Berdal and Malone, *Greed and Grievance,* pp. 137–153; Michael Pugh, "Postwar Political Economy in Bosnia and Herzegovina: The Spoils of Peace," *Global Governance* 8, no. 4: 467–482; Jonathan Goodhand, "Afghanistan," in M. Pugh and N. Cooper, *War Economies in a Regional Context: Challenges of Transformation* (Boulder: Lynne Rienner, 2004), pp. 45–89.

60. See www.worldbank.org/afr/ccproj.

61. North and South Kivu provinces are mostly inhabited by Bafuliro, Bahavu, Bahunde, Banande, Banyanga, Bashi, Bavira, Banyabwisha (Banyarwanda), Banyamulenge, and Barundi. Except for the last three groups, most of these people are culturally similar. All the groups share a customary system of power based on the Bwami association, which involves a complex hierarchical system based on age and wealth. The innovation of most tribal principalities in the Great Lakes region was to develop elaborate rules of succession and ascension to the throne, royal funerals based on sophisticated systems linked to land, and royal seals and supernatural symbols that linked the people to their prince, or Mwami. A common ancestor was replaced by the cult of sacred kings who levied tribute annually either in the form of agricultural products or livestock. Banyamulenge also paid annual tributes to the Bafuliro and Bavira chiefs. See L. Viane, "L'organisation politique des Bahunde," *Kongo Oversee* 18 (1952): 8–32; also Bashizi Cirhagarhula, "Mythe hamite, formations étatiques et acculturations interlacustres," in Jean-Baptiste Ntahokaja et al., eds., *La civilisation ancienne des peuples des Grands Lacs: Colloque de Bujumbura, 4–10 September 1979* (Paris: Editions Karthals, 1981), pp. 235–236. For analysis of tribute systems, see Jean-Claude Willame, *Banyarwanda et Banyamulenge: Violences éthniques et gestion de l'identitaire au Kivu* (Brussels: Institut africain–CEDAF; Paris: L'Harmattan, 1997), p. 85.

62. See, for example, Alvaro de Soto and Graciana del Castillo's analysis of contradictions between UN and IFI reconstruction strategies for El Salvador in "Obstacles to Peacebuilding," *Foreign Policy* 94 (spring 1994): 69–83.

63. Elizabeth Cousins, "From Missed Opportunities to Overcompensation: Implementing the Dayton Agreement on Bosnia,"in Stedman, Rothchild, and Cousens, *Ending Civil Wars,* pp. 541–545.

6

Conclusion

Our findings regarding the Congo War contribute to and complement other research on economic agendas in civil wars, especially that of the International Peace Academy's Program on Economic Agendas in Civil Wars (EACW)—under whose auspices this book has been produced.

Like other conflicts analyzed by the EACW and other research projects, economic interests were not the main factor in the *onset* of the Congo War.[1] Long-standing political and social grievances interacted with economic interests to motivate major rebel groups. Economic interests were also not the main factor that led foreign governments to intervene. To be sure, the economic agendas of foreign belligerents eventually became a prominent part of the conflict and were an obscured part of the peace process, but they emerged as a function of war; interstate war did not occur as a result of economic interests. This is not entirely the case at the local level, where grievances related to economic opportunities have long caused tensions that periodically result in the kinds of local armed conflicts that contribute to the "Congo wars" phenomenon.

Even in the closing stages of the conflict, economic agendas have not been more important than other interests. Evidence for this is the behavior of foreign actors in the wake of the peace agreement. Ugandan and Zimbabwean governments and militaries (and individuals within these organizations) have invested heavily in their commercial activities in the DRC and stand the most to lose by withdrawing. Yet it is precisely these countries that have undertaken the most extensive disengagement. By contrast, Rwanda's military activities were mostly financed by its economic interests, and an RPA withdrawal would mean that it would not have to continue those activities. Yet Rwanda remains both military and economically engaged, primarily because of continuing security concerns caused by the inability of the DRC government and the MONUC to disarm Hutu militias and secure its Congolese frontier. Clearly, notwithstanding the importance of economic interests for these actors, economic agendas remain only one dimension among others.

It is important that holistic (multidimensional) analyses of conflicts are applied to the Congo War and are extended to understanding the travails of its peace process. As Karen Ballentine and Jake Sherman have observed, the importance of divisible economic interests—that is, economic interests that can be atomized—can actually make conflicts primarily based on such interests more amenable to resolution than conflicts for which economic dimensions are only one of many.[2] The Congo War has been difficult to resolve precisely because it is *not* just about economic interests. As argued in Chapter 4, unsuccessful peace initiatives for the Congo War were not derailed because of economic interests. These accords (like the final Pretoria accord) never fundamentally addressed the economic dimensions of the conflict anyway. The Lusaka agreement foundered over power-sharing formulas that were politically unacceptable to Laurent Kabila, and the Sun City talks foundered over security issues. Economic interests may contribute to the perpetuation of conflict by either enabling combatants to survive or providing a reason to continue fighting, but they do not necessarily prevent peace talks, ceasefires, or even final peace agreements involving national-level actors.

Because tensions regarding natural resources in the DRC are embedded in historical patterns of governance by the state, it is not sufficient to simply strengthen state capacity or introduce greater transparency in decisionmaking and fiscal matters—although these may help mitigate against conditions in which rebellion and predatory and criminal economic behavior flourish. The relationship between authorities, the resources they control, and the populace is at the root of the Congo War, and until this relationship changes, prospects for peace will remain fraught. This observation is supported by the findings of other studies that confirm that "critical governance failure by the state appears to be the mediating variable between resource abundance and the risk of armed conflict."[3] Alone, and even together, UN missions and the international community cannot reverse "governance failure" in relation to managing natural resources. They can, however, have some influence over the behavior of foreign governments and companies participating in the exploitation of natural resources. *Primary* responsibility for changing patterns of governance—or not changing them—must rest with Congolese leaders, although there is little indication that the current leaders are interested in making such changes. In keeping with the argument throughout the book that understanding and addressing pre-conflict patterns of governance are critical to long-term resolution of the Congo wars, it may be useful for peace accords to include provisions for restructuring patterns of governance once ceasefires are signed. Examples might include the development of mutually agreed rules for the sale, transfer, and use of state- and customary-owned lands and sub-surface rights, as well as mutually acceptable institutions to regulate these rules. Such measures may well delay the signing of peace accords, but they may also improve the chances that the root causes of grievances and predatory and criminal behavior related to natural resources are eventually addressed.

Our study confirms EACW findings regarding the relationship between resource wealth and armed conflict, although the Congo War is more nuanced in one important respect. The book's analysis supports the finding that abundant resources that furnish easy rents to the state may undermine the state in the long term. However, the EACW project's finding that "mismanagement of resource wealth may create grievances that—particularly when fused with a history of ethno-secessionist ten-dencies—may become permissive factors for armed conflict" is insuffi-ciently nuanced for the DRC case.[4] Especially in eastern DRC, many ethno-secessionist tendencies cannot be separated from the state's man-agement of resources. Thus, there was no "fusing" of two different phe-nomena; in the DRC, they are most often one and the same, and it is critical that scholars, policymakers, and humanitarians understand this.

The finding, from other research, that profits from natural resources can shape the character and duration of conflict,[5] especially efforts to end conflict, was confirmed by Grignon in Chapter 4. A consequence of the effect of profits from natural resources is that wars that start as polit-ical rebellions can "mutate over time as economic considerations become equally or even more important to some combatants than politi-cal aspirations."[6] Michael L. Ross argues that the Angolan conflict fits into this category;[7] the Congo War does as well.

The book's analysis of rebel factions and the reasons for their multi-plication provides evidence in support of George Downs and Stephen Stedman's finding that the two main factors in failed peace implementa-tion—and failed peace implementation is, arguably, what exists in east-ern DRC—are the proliferation of combatant parties and ongoing access by combatants to natural resources.[8]

The book has produced an open finding with regard to the success of the MONUC and associated reconstruction efforts. Certainly the large number of war-related deaths from ongoing conflict in eastern DRC suggests that this may well be the price and product of a failed intervention on the part of the MONUC. Indeed, the MONUC has all the hallmarks of failure: inadequate resources given the size and complexity of the DRC, the lack of a great power or regional hegemon with a binding interest in resolving the conflict, an inability to disarm and demobilize all belligerents, and inadequate attention to economic interests and grievances. However, this study has documented some significant achievements of the MONUC. First is the fact that it exists: with approximately 14,000 troops it is the largest UN peacekeeping intervention ever. Second, its presence is the major reason interstate and national-level conflict has been quelled. Third, its support has been a key factor in the DRC remaining whole. Scholars often question the usefulness of maintaining existing state borders in Africa, but Congolese—and Africans in general—seem to agree that this is what they want. Fourth, it oversees a DDRRR program that is addressing some important issues, although progress has been fitful and slow.

Policy Lessons

Our analyses and findings regarding economic agendas have, in turn, produced some lessons for policymakers. Some of these are generic and have already been well identified elsewhere, including the importance of: improving governance and state capacity to prevent conflict; better regulation of the commodities that sustain belligerents or provide a reason for their continuing hostilities; better targeting of criminal elements involved in conflict production and marketing; identifying the culpability of states—in addition to that of their rebel adversaries—in the violent exploitation of natural resources; regional approaches to tackling criminal behavior and economic networks; and ensuring that efforts to constrict illicit natural resource exploitation minimize harm to civilian populations.[9]

This study has produced some additional policy lessons that are less evident from research into other conflicts. First, outside actors *are* able to influence what issues get tabled during peace negotiations, as evidenced by the effect of the UN Panel of Experts' reports into the economic dimensions of the Congo War. Even though economic dimensions were not subsequently addressed in any meaningful sense, and even though the reports reflected the biases and interests of their Security Council sponsors, the importance of the UN as a forum in which governments have to account for themselves when publicly exposed was clearly demonstrated. This process can, in turn, create opportunities for the international community to shape peace negotiations and ensure that they focus on certain issues.

Second, the salience of economic interests vis-à-vis other interests for certain actors, namely national-level actors, is different from that of regional or local actors. This is because national actors can parlay their military or economic influence into political power at the state level—something that would probably enable them to continue their control over economic interests or to obtain new opportunities anyway. Subnational actors do not have the same ability to use their military or economic influence at the national level. Peace accords that offer incentives to subnational actors similar to those for national-level actors are therefore more likely to be brokered and to succeed. Federal systems make this easier, because they can offer more attractive incentives at the subnational level. If a federal system is not in place or final political arrangements are yet to be worked out, it will be harder to get local belligerents to participate in peace accords. This has important consequences for mediators (who need to distinguish between different levels of conflict in order to select the most effective incentives and sanctions) and for peace operations (which need to develop and select programs for reconstruction most likely to address grievances and restructure the conditions that gave rise to conflict).

Third, a regional approach to conflict is essential if the networks that facilitated the licit and illicit production and marketing of primary commodities are to be better regulated. In the DRC case, it would be useful if African regional institutions could take the lead in this respect. However, despite the existence of four organizations with interests in the DRC (the AU, the SADC, the Common Market of East and Southern Africa, and the Economic Community of Central African States), they have proved insufficient to mediate peace or direct reconstruction efforts. With few exceptions,[10] African multilateral organizations have proved ineffective at postconflict reconstruction, although they have had better success with mediation and peacekeeping. One reason for this is their lack of resources. Another is that their overlapping mandates and memberships hinder the creation of both uniform regional policies and clear divisions of labor (such as for defense, trade, or development). Such multiplicity has resulted in "duplication, competition, wasted resources and inefficiency, and has slowed progress towards the achievement of regional goals."[11]

A major reason for the ineffectiveness of African regional institutions in the DRC case is that they were never intended for this purpose. The lack of resources provided by member states and the occasional outright undermining of previously agreed regional positions by some members suggest that members have no real commitment to creating multilateral institutions with the capacity to successfully intervene in a member state. The four regional organizations mentioned also lack a hegemon with sufficient interest in the DRC to ensure that the organization is suitably resourced and committed to intervene. South Africa is economically dominant within the SADC, but the split within the organization in 1998 over military support for the Kabila government indicates that South African political power is not unfettered. Therefore, while the AU, the SADC, or NEPAD may be able to play a constructive role in the DRC and other conflicts in the future, peacemakers must be realistic about the capacity of regional African institutions to intervene and the degree of political support for intervention from member governments. In the DRC case, implementation of peace and reconstruction efforts will of necessity probably remain in the hands of the United Nations.

Fourth, it is worth contrasting the varying effects of different actors' strategies for exploiting natural resources. The importance of large parastatals and foreign mining companies in areas such as in Katanga has resulted in government strategies for revenue raising that are more predictable, and much less bloody, than the strategies of rebel organizations with interests in coltan or diamonds. This suggests that peace efforts for conflicts involving mineral resources could usefully involve foreign mining companies and parastatals. Large mining institutions may inhibit the ability of individual local and regional leaders to manipulate production and trade. Direct involvement in peace negotiations by mining corporations could also better guarantee revenues to the state. There are risks to this approach: the general political influence of corporate actors in postconflict situations would inevitably increase; and artisanal miners may also become redundant, causing unemployment and hardship, although it may be possible to organize some kind of compensation or employment arrangement.

Fifth, notwithstanding any apparent progress at the national level, local conflicts must be addressed and integrated into the peace process—although what factors need to be considered when doing this and precisely when this should happen remain open questions we have not answered. In the case of eastern DRC, including North Kivu, South Kivu, and Ituri, one solution may be to hold a conference attended by all Congolese factions to identify solutions to the grievances of that region, especially regarding land and mining concessions. A second challenge for the region is the continuing grievances over citizenship, but this is a difficult area for the international community to become involved in, because by definition citizenship issues must be dealt with at the national level through the reform of national legislation.

Finally, and in keeping with the book's finding that understanding and addressing preconflict patterns of governance are critical to long-term resolution of the Congo wars, peace accords should ideally include provisions for restructuring patterns of governance once ceasefires are signed. The policy challenge is to identify how outside mediators and the international community can influence what specifically gets tabled for negotiation during peace talks, especially if the international community is excluded as in the DRC case.

The book began by asking when economic interests should be introduced into peace negotiations or made the focus of reconstruction efforts for multidimensional conflicts. This remains an open question, although in the case of the Congo War, the nature of belligerents' economic interests and their fluctuating and relative importance vis-à-vis other interests over the course of the conflict, the peace process, and reconstruction efforts should now be far clearer. Priorities for further research on this issue have also been illuminated. First is the need for additional policy research on rebel grievances as advocated by David Malone and Heiko Nitzschke.[12] Chapters 2 and 3 drew on original field research by Tatiana Carayannis on the MLC, Frank Van Acker and Koen Vlassenroot on the Mai Mai, and various authors associated with the Pole Institute on local conflicts in eastern DRC—all valuable contributions to scholarly analysis of rebel interests. However, much additional research is required on the social and political grievances of Congolese rebel groups, particularly how and why these grievances interact with economic interests and vice versa. Second, research into the optimal timing for introducing economic interests into peace negotiations is critical for the development of general models or theories of negotiation for civil wars involving economic agendas. Calculating and publicizing the death and destruction caused by different actors at all levels of multilevel conflicts may help identify what subconflicts, and therefore what interests, should be addressed first. Questions remain as to why major parties would agree to consider such conflicts, and what the international community could do to help achieve this outcome. But in the DRC case, early analysis and identification could have made local conflicts in eastern DRC an earlier priority for resolution.

Notes

1. See Karen Ballentine, "Beyond Greed and Grievance: Reconsidering the Economic Dynamics of Armed Conflict," in Karen Ballentine and Jake Sherman, eds., *The Political Economy of Armed Conflict: Beyond Greed and Grievance* (Boulder, Colo.: Lynne Rienner, 2003), pp. 259–283; Karen Ballentine and Heiko Nitzschke, "Beyond Greed and Grievance: Policy Lessons from Studies in the Political Economy of Armed Conflict," an International Peace Academy Policy Report (New York: IPA, October 2003); Wayne E. Nafziger and Juha Auvinen, *Economic Development, Inequality, and War: Humanitarian Emergencies in Developing Countries* (Basingstoke, England: Palgrave Macmillan, 2003).

2. Ballentine and Sherman, *The Political Economy of Armed Conflict*, pp. 273–274.

3. David M. Malone and Heiko Nitzschke, "Economic Agendas in Civil Wars: What We Know, What We Need to Know," Discussion Paper No. 2005/07, April 2005, World Institute for Development Economics Research, p. 5. Also see Charles Cater, "The Political Economy of Conflict and UN Intervention: Rethinking the Critical Cases of Africa," in Ballentine and Sherman, *The Political Economy of Armed Conflict*, pp. 19–45; James D. Fearon and David D. Laitin, "Ethnicity, Insurgency, and Civil War," *American Political Science Review* 97, no. 1 (2003): 75–90; Nafziger and Auvinen, *Economic Development, Inequality, and War*; Frances Stewart, "Horizontal Inequalities as a Source of Conflict," in F. Osler Hampson and D. M. Malone, eds., *From Reaction to Conflict Prevention: Opportunities for the UN System* (Boulder, Colo.: Lynne Rienner, 2002), pp. 105–136; Jeffrey D. Sachs and Andrew M. Warner, "The Curse of Natural Resources," *European Economic Review* 45 (2001): 827–838.

4. Malone and Nitzschke, "Economic Agendas in Civil Wars," p. 5.

5. Ballentine, "Beyond Greed and Grievance."

6. Malone and Nitzschke, "Economic Agendas in Civil Wars," p. 6.

7. Michael L. Ross, "How Does Natural Resource Wealth Influence Civil War? Evidence from 13 Cases," *International Organization* 58, no. 1 (2004): 35–67.

8. George Downs and Stephen J. Stedman, "Evaluation Issues in Peace Implementation," in Stephen J. Stedman, Donald Rothchild, and Elizabeth M. Cousens, eds., *Ending Civil Wars: The Implementation of Peace Agreements* (Boulder, Colo.: Lynne Rienner, 2002), pp. 43–69.

9. Malone and Nitzschke, "Economic Agendas in Civil Wars"; Michael Pugh and Neil Cooper, with Jonathan Goodhand, *War Economies in a Regional Context: Challenges of Transformation* (Boulder, Colo.: Lynne Rienner, 2004); Ballentine and Sherman, *The Political Economy of Armed Conflict*; Ballentine and Nitzschke, "Beyond Greed and Grievance"; Stedman, Rothchild, and Cousens, *Ending Civil Wars*.

10. These include the Inter-Governmental Authority on Development, which helped negotiate a ceasefire and peace accord between belligerents in the Sudanese Civil War (Ciru Mwaura and Susanne Schmeidl, eds., *Early Warning and Conflict Management in the Horn of Africa* [Lawrenceville, N.J.: Red Sea

Press, 2002]); and the Economic Community of West African States, whose successes and failures at peacekeeping and peace enforcement in West Africa are directly related to the interests of Nigeria, the regional hegemon (Adekeye Adebajo, *Building Peace in West Africa: Liberia, Sierra Leone, and Guinea-Bissau* [Boulder, Colo.: Lynne Rienner, 2002]). The African Union's peacekeeping missions in Darfur, Sudan, and in Côte d'Ivoire also hold promise—see International Crisis Group, "The AU's Mission in Darfur: Bridging the Gaps," Africa Briefing No. 28, July 6, 2005; "Côte d'Ivoire: The Worst May Be Yet to Come," Africa Briefing No. 90, March 24, 2005).

   11. Ciru Mwaura, "Lessons for Regional Conflict Management and Conflict Prevention" (manuscript, Oxfam Great Britain, 2004), p. 15.

   12. Malone and Nitzschke, "Economic Agendas in Civil Wars," p. 5.

Acronyms

ADF	Allied Defence Forces, Ugandan
AFDL	Alliance des Forces Démocratiques pour la Libération du Congo-Zaire
ANR	Agence National de Renseignements
ASD	Association for the Salvation of the Dialogue
AU	African Union
CCP	Chad-Cameroon Petroleum Development and Pipeline Project
DDR	disarmament, demobilization, and reintegration
DDRRR	disarmament, demobilization, repatriation, resettlement, and reintegration
DRC	Democratic Republic of Congo
EACW	Economic Agendas in Civil Wars
EIU	Economist Intelligence Unit
FAC	Forces Armées Congolaises
FAR	Forces Armées Rwandaises
FARDC	Forces Armées de la République Démocratique du Congo
FAZ	Forces Armées Zairoises
FDD	Forces de Défense de la Démocratie
FDLR	Force Démocratique de Libération du Rwanda
FLC	Front de Libération du Congo
GDP	gross domestic product
HRW	Human Rights Watch
ICD	Inter-Congolese Dialogue
ICG	International Crisis Group
ICST	International Committee to Support the Transition
IDA	International Development Association

IDI	International Diamond Industries
IFI	international financial institution
IFRA	Institut Français de Recherche en Afrique
IGAD	Inter-Governmental Authority on Development
IMC	Implementation and Monitoring Commission
IMF	International Monetary Fund
IPA	International Peace Academy
IRIN	Integrated Regional Information Networks
KPCS	Kimberly Process Certification Scheme
LDF	Local Defence Forces
MAGRIVI	Mutuelle Agricole des Virunga
MDRP	Multi-Country Demobilization and Reintegration Program
MLC	Mouvement pour la Libération du Congo
MONUC	Mission de l'Organisation des Nations Unies au République Démocratique du Congo (UN Observer Mission to the Democratic Republic of the Congo)
MSF	Médecins sans Frontières
NEPAD	New Partnership for Africa's Development
NGO	nongovernmental organization
OAU	Organization of African Unity
OCHA	Office for the Coordination of Humanitarian Affairs
OFICD	Office of the Facilitator for the Inter-Congolese Dialogue
OSCE	Organization for Security and Co-operation in Europe
PPRD	Parti pour la Reconstruction et le Développement
PRERP	Post-Reunification Economic Recovery Project
PRGF	Poverty Reduction and Growth Facility
RCD	Rassemblement Congolais pour la Démocratie
RCD-ML	Rassemblement Congolais pour la Démocratie– Mouvement de Libération
RMLC	Revolutionary Movement for the Liberation of Congo
RPA	Rwandan Patriotic Army
RPF	Rwandan Patriotic Front
SADC	Southern African Development Community
SLORC	State Law and Order Restoration Committee
SMP	Staff-Monitored Program
SNC	Sovereign National Conference
TPD	Tous pour la Paix et le Développement
UDPS	Union pour la Démocratie et le Progrès Social
UNICEF	United Nations Children's Fund
UNDP	United Nations Development Programme
UNHCR	UN High Commissioner for Refugees

UNITA	União Nacional para a Independência Total de Angola
UPC	Union des Patriotes Congolais
UPDF	Uganda People's Defence Force
WHO	World Health Organization
WIDER	World Institute for Development Economics Research
WNBF	West Nile Bank Front
ZANU-PF	Zimbabwe African National Union–Patriotic Front
ZDF	Zimbabwe Defence Forces

Bibliography

Adebajo, Adekeye, *Building Peace in West Africa: Liberia, Sierra Leone, and Guinea-Bissau* (Boulder, Colo.: Lynne Rienner, 2002).

Africa Confidential, "Congo-Kinshasa: Soldiers Go, Plunderers Stay," 43, no. 21, October 25, 2002.

———, "Soldiers of Misfortune," 41, no. 18, September 15, 2000, p. 7.

———, "Glittering Prizes II," 41, no. 12, June 9, 2000, p. 8.

———, "Glittering Prizes from the War," 41, no. 11, May 26, 2000, p. 2.

———, "Rhodies to the Rescue," 40, no. 22, November 5, 1999, p. 6.

———, "Mining for Trouble," 37, no. 25, December 13, 1996, pp. 5–6.

African Research Bulletin, "Coltan," July 16–August 15, 2004, p. 16204.

———, "Cruel By-Products of War," June 16–July 15, 2004, p. 15936.

———, "Zaire: Nationalization Measures," November 15–December 14, 1973, pp. 2946–2947.

African Rights, *DRC: The Cycle of Conflict; Which Way Out in the Kivus?* (London: African Rights, December 2000).

Agence France-Presse, "Lubumbashi Massacres Kill 100," May 22, 1991.

Akitoby, Bernadin, and Matthias Cinyabuguma, "Sources of Growth in the Democratic Republic of the Congo: An Econometric Approach." In Jean A. P. Clément, ed., *Postconflict Economics in Sub-Saharan Africa: Lessons from the Democratic Republic of the Congo* (Washington, D.C.: International Monetary Fund, 2004).

Amnesty International, *Deadly Alliances in Congolese Forests* (New York: Amnesty International, 1997).

Associated Press, "U.N. Sees 'More and More' Signs That Rwandan Troops Are in Congo," December 3, 2004.

———, "Republic of Congo, Expelled from World Diamond Trade for Alleged Smuggling, Signs Diamond Pact with Neighbors," November 24, 2004.

Ball, Nicole, "Demobilizing and Reintegrating Soldiers." In Krishna Kumar, ed., *Rebuilding Societies After Civil War: Critical Roles for International Assistance* (Boulder, Colo.: Lynne Rienner, 1997).

Ballentine, Karen, "Beyond Greed and Grievance: Reconsidering the Economic Dynamics of Armed Conflict." In Karen Ballentine and Jake Sherman, eds.,

The Political Economy of Armed Conflict: Beyond Greed and Grievance (Boulder, Colo.: Lynne Rienner, 2003), pp. 259–283.

Ballentine, Karen, and Heiko Nitzschke, "Beyond Greed and Grievance: Policy Lessons from Studies in the Political Economy of Armed Conflict," an International Peace Academy Policy Report (New York: IPA, October 2003).

Ballentine, Karen, and Jake Sherman, eds., *The Political Economy of Armed Conflict: Beyond Greed and Grievance* (Boulder, Colo.: Lynne Rienner, 2003).

Bannon, Ian, and Paul Collier, eds., *Natural Resources and Violent Conflict: Options and Actions* (Washington, D.C.: World Bank, 2004).

Berdal, Mats, and David Malone, eds., *Greed and Grievance: Economic Agendas in Civil Wars* (Boulder, Colo.: Lynne Rienner, 2000).

Boshoff, Henri, and Martin Rupiya, "Delegates, Dialogue and Desperadoes: The ICD and the DRC Peace Process," *African Studies Review* 12, no. 3 (March 2003): 212–218.

Bouvier, Paule, in collaboration with Francesca Bomboko, *Le dialogue inter-congolais: Anatomie d'une négociation à la lisière du chaos; Contribution à la théorie de la négociation* (Tervuren, Belgium: Institut africain–CEDAF, 2003).

Buell, Raymond Leslie, *The Native Problem in Africa,* vol. 2 (New York: Macmillan, 1928).

Bureau d'Études, du Recherche et du Consulting International, *Rapport d'évaluation: 7ème semaine du Dialogue Intercongolais* (Kinshasa and Sun City, South Africa: BERCI, April 8–14, 2002).

Callaghy, Thomas, "From Reshaping to Resizing a Failing State? The Case of the Congo/Zaire" (manuscript, 1998).

———, *The State-Society Struggle: Zaire in Comparative Perspective* (New York: Columbia University Press, 1984).

Carayannis, Tatiana, "Hybrid Wars, Conflict Networks, and Multilateral Responses: The Congo Wars, 1996–2004," Ph.D. diss., City University of New York Graduate Center, forthcoming 2006.

———, "Rebels with a Cause? A Study of the Mouvement de Libération du Congo," paper delivered at the African Studies Association annual conference, Washington, D.C., December 5–8, 2002.

Cater, Charles, "The Political Economy of Conflict and UN Intervention: Rethinking the Critical Cases of Africa." In Karen Ballentine and Jake Sherman, eds., *The Political Economy of Armed Conflict: Beyond Greed and Grievance* (Boulder, Colo.: Lynne Rienner, 2003), pp. 19–45.

Cirhagarhula, Bashizi, "Mythe hamite, formations étatiques et acculturation interlacustres." In Jean-Baptiste Ntahokaja et al., eds., *La civilisation ancienne des peuples des Grands Lacs: Colloque de Bujumbura, September 4–10, 1979* (Paris: Editions Karthals, 1981).

Clark, John F., "Explaining Ugandan Intervention in Congo: Evidence and Interpretations," *Journal of Modern African Studies* 39, no. 2 (2001): 261–287.

———, "Zaire: The Bankruptcy of the Extraction State." In Leonardo A. Villalón and Philip A. Huxtable, eds., *The African State at a Critical*

Juncture: Between Disintegration and Reconfiguration (Boulder, Colo.: Lynne Rienner, 1998).

Clément, Jean A. P., "The Democratic Republic of the Congo: Lessons and Challenges for a Country Emerging From War." In Jean A. P. Clément, ed., *Postconflict Economics in Sub-Saharan Africa: Lessons from the Democratic Republic of the Congo* (Washington, D.C.: International Monetary Fund, 2004).

CNN.com, "Congo Leader Kabila Vows to Crush Rebels," August 4, 1998.

————, "Kinshasa Under Curfew as Congo Army Revolts Against Kabila," August 3, 1998.

Coakley, George J., *The Mineral Industry of Congo (Kinshasa)*, U.S. Geological Survey (Washington, D.C.: U.S. Bureau of Mines, 2002).

Colletta, Nat J., Markus Kostner, and Ingo Wiederhofer, *The Transition from War to Peace in Sub-Saharan Africa* (Washington, D.C.: U.S. Peace Institute, 1996).

Collier, Paul, "Doing Well Out of War: An Economic Perspective." In Mats Berdal and David M. Malone, eds., *Greed and Grievance: Economic Agendas in Civil* Wars (Boulder, Colo.: Lynne Rienner, 2000).

Compagnon, David, "'Mugabe and Partners (PVT) LTD' ou l'investissement politique du champ économique," *Politique Africaine* 81 (March 2001): 101–119.

Cooper, Neil, "State Collapse as Business: The Role of Conflict Trade and the Emerging Control Agenda," *Development and Change* 33, no. 55 (2002): 935–955.

Cosete, Joanne, *The War Within the War: Sexual Violence Against Women and Girls in Eastern Congo* (New York: Human Rights Watch, 2002).

Cousins, Elizabeth, "From Missed Opportunities to Overcompensation: Implementing the Dayton Agreement on Bosnia." In Stephen J. Stedman, Donald Rothchild, and Elizabeth M. Cousens, eds., *Ending Civil Wars: The Implementation of Peace Agreements* (Boulder, Colo.: Lynne Rienner, 2002).

Cunningham, Larry D., "Columbium (Niobium) and Tantalum." In U.S. Geological Survey's *Minerals Yearbook* (Washington, D.C.: U.S. Bureau of Mines, 2003).

Cuvelier, Jeroen, and Tim Raeymaekers, *European Companies and the Coltan Trade: An Update*, Part 2 (Brussels: International Peace Information Service, 2002).

————, *Supporting the War Economy in the DRC: European Companies and the Coltan Trade: Five Case Studies* (Brussels: International Peace Information Service, 2002).

Democratic Republic of Congo, Government of, *Rapport Annuel* (Kinshasa: Banque Centrale, 2002).

De Soto, Alvaro, and Graciana del Castillo, "Obstacles to Peacebuilding," *Foreign Policy* 94 (spring 1994): 69–83.

De Villers, Gauthier, Jean-Claude Willame, Jean Omasombo Tshonda, and Eric Kennes, *République démocratique du Congo: Chronique politique de l'en-tre-deux-guerres, Octobre 1996–Juillet 1998*, Cahiers Africains 35–36 (Tervuren, Belgium: Institut africain–CEDAF, 1998).

De Witte, Ludo, *The Assassination of Lumumba* (London: Verso, 2001).

Dietrich, Chris, *The Commercialisation of Military Deployment in Africa* (Pretoria: Institute for Security Studies, January 26, 2001).

Downs, George, and Stephen J. Stedman, "Evaluation Issues in Peace Implementation." In Stephen J. Stedman, Donald Rothchild, and Elizabeth M. Cousens, eds., *Ending Civil Wars: The Implementation of Peace Agreements* (Boulder, Colo.: Lynne Rienner, 2002).

Drèze, Jean, and Amartya Sen, "Introduction." In Jean Drèze, Amartya Sen, and Athar Husain, eds., *The Political Economy of Hunger* (Oxford: Clarendon Press, 1995).

Duffield, Mark, "Post-modern Conflict: Warlords, Post-adjustment States and Private Protection," *Civil Wars* 1, no. 1 (spring 1998): 65–102.

Dunn, Kevin, "A Survival Guide to Kinshasa: Lessons of the Father Passed Down to the Son." In John F. Clark, *The African Stakes of the Congo War* (New York: Palgrave Macmillan, 2002), pp. 53–74.

Economist Intelligence Unit, *DRC Country Report* (London: EIU, May 2001).

———, *Zimbabwe Country Report* (London: EIU, 2000).

———, *DRC Country Report*, (London: EIU, February 1999).

———, *DRC Country Report* (London: EIU, November 1998).

Emizet, Kisangani N. F., "Conflict in the Democratic Republic of Congo: A Mosaic of Insurgent Groups," *International Journal on World Peace* 20, no. 3 (September 2003).

———, "Confronting Leaders at the Apex of the State," *African Studies Review* 41, no. 1 (April 1998): 99–137.

———, *Zaire After Mobutu: A Case of a Humanitarian Emergency* (Helsinki: World Institute for Development Economics Research, 1997).

European Union, *Stratégie de coopération et programme indicatif, République Démocratique du Congo, 2003–2007* (Brussels: European Union, 2003).

Fearon, James D., and David D. Laitin, "Ethnicity, Insurgency, and Civil War," *American Political Science Review* 97, no. 1 (2003): 75–90.

Financial Gazette (Harare), "Government Presses DRC to Pay $100bn Debt in Forex," January 9, 2003.

Frustone, Joël, "The Forced Repatriation of Congolese Refugees Living in Rwanda" (Washington, D.C.: U.S. Committee for Refugees, December 16, 2002).

Furlonger, David, "Ventures into the Interior," *Financial Mail* (Johannesburg), May 28, 1999, pp. 58–60.

Goodhand, Jonathan, "Afghanistan." In M. Pugh and N. Cooper, *War Economies in a Regional Context: Challenges of Transformation* (Boulder, Colo.: Lynne Rienner, 2004), pp. 45–89.

Gourevitch, Philip, *We Wish to Inform You That Tomorrow We Will Be Killed with Our Families: Stories from Rwanda* (New York: Harper, 1998).

Grant, J. Andrew, and Ian Taylor, "Global Governance and Conflict Diamonds: The Kimberley Process and the Quest for Clean Gems," *The Round Table* 93, no. 375: 385–401.

Havenne, Émile, "La deuxième guerre d'Afrique centrale." In Filip Reyntjens and Stefaan Marysse, eds., *L'Afrique des Grands Lacs: Annuaire 2000–2001* (Antwerp: CERGLA, 2001), pp. 143–174.

Hochschild, Adam, *King Leopold's Ghost: A Story of Greed, Terror, and Heroism in Colonial Africa* (Boston: Houghton Mifflin, 1998).

Human Rights Watch, *Chaos in Eastern Congo: U.N. Action Needed Now* (New York: HRW, 2002).

———, *Eastern Congo Ravaged* (New York: HRW, 2001).

———, *Reluctant Recruits: Children and Adults Forcibly Recruited for Military Service in North Kivu* (New York: HRW, 2001).

———, *Casualties of War: Civilians, Rule of Law, and Democratic Freedoms* (New York: HRW, 1999).

Integrated Regional Information Networks, "DRC: EU Suspends Projects in North Kivu," March 2, 2005.

———, "DRC: Bemba-Led Rebel Group Signs Accord with Mayi-Mayi," March 29, 2001.

International Committee of the Red Cross, *War, Money, and Survival* (Geneva: ICRC, 2002).

International Crisis Group, *The AU's Mission in Darfur: Bridging the Gaps*, Africa Briefing No. 28 (Nairobi: ICG, July 6, 2005).

———, *The Congo's Transition is Failing: Crisis in the Kivus*, Africa Report No. 91 (Nairobi: ICG, March 30, 2005).

———, *Côte d'Ivoire: The Worst May Be Yet to Come*, Africa Briefing No. 90 (Nairobi: ICG, March 24, 2005).

———, *Back to the Brink in the Congo*, Africa Briefing No. 21 (Nairobi: ICG, December 17, 2004).

———, *Pulling Back from the Brink in the Congo*, Africa Briefing No. 18 (Nairobi: ICG, July 7, 2004).

———, *The Kivus: The Crucible of the Congo Conflict*, Africa Report No. 56 (Nairobi: ICG, January 24, 2003).

———, *Storm Clouds over Sun City: The Urgent Need to Recast the Congolese Peace Process,* Africa Report No. 44 (Nairobi: ICG, March 14, 2002).

———, *Rwanda/Uganda: A Dangerous War of Nerves*, Africa Briefing No. 7 (Nairobi: ICG, December 21, 2001).

———, *Le dialogue intercongolais: Poker menteur ou négociation politique?* Africa Report No. 37 (Nairobi: ICG, November 16, 2001).

———, *Scramble for the Congo: Anatomy of an Ugly War*, Africa Report No. 26 (Nairobi: ICG, December 20, 2000).

———, *Uganda and Rwanda: Friends or Enemies?* Africa Report No.14 (Nairobi: ICG, May 4, 2000).

———, *The Agreement on a Cease-fire in the Democratic Republic of Congo: An Analysis of the Agreement and Prospects for Peace*, DRC Report No. 5 (Nairobi: ICG, August 20, 1999).

International Monetary Fund, "DRC: Request for a Three-Year Arrangement Under the Poverty Reduction and Growth Facility and the First Annual Program—Staff Report" (Washington, D.C.: IMF, July 2002).

———, "DRC: 2001 Article IV Consultation and Discussions on Staff-Monitoring Program" (Washington, D.C: IMF, July 2001).

International Rescue Committee and the Burnet Institute, "Mortality Rates in the Democratic Republic of Congo: Results from a Nationwide Survey, Conducted April–July 2004" (New York: International Rescue Committee,

December 2004).

Johnson, Dominic, "Shifting Sands: Oil Exploration in the Rift Valley and the Congo Conflict" (Goma, DRC: Pole Institute, March 2003).

Kahiya, Vincent, "No Diamond Cheques for Zimbabwe in the DRC," *Zimbabwe Independent* (Harare), March 10, 2000, p. 1.

Kaldor, Mary, *New and Old Wars: Organized Violence in a Global Era* (Stanford, Calif.: Stanford University Press, 1999).

Kennes, Erik, "Footnotes to the Mining Story," *Review of African Political Economy* 29, no. 93/94 (2002): 601–607.

———, "Le secteur minier au Congo: 'Déconnexion' et descente aux enfers." In Filip Reyntjens and Stefaan Marysse, eds., *L'Afrique des Grands Lacs: Annuaire 1999–2000* (Antwerp: Centre d'Étude de la Région des Grands Lacs d'Afrique, 2000), pp. 299–343.

Kickmeyer, Ellen, "Congo Cancels Israeli-Diamond Supply," Associated Press, April 21, 2001.

Kimberley Process, www.kimberleyprocess.com.

Kostner, Markus, Ely Dieng, and Andriaan Verheul, "The Long Road to Demilitarization." In Jean A. P. Clément, ed., *Postconflict Economics in Sub-Saharan Africa: Lessons from the Democratic Republic of the Congo* (Washington, D.C.: International Monetary Fund, 2004).

Koyame, Mungbalemwe, and John F. Clark, "The Economic Impact of the Congo War." In John F. Clark, ed., *The African Stakes of the Congo War* (New York: Palgrave Macmillan, 2002).

Le Billon, Philippe, "Fuelling War: Natural Resources and Armed Conflict," Adelphi Paper No. 373 (London: International Institute for Strategic Studies, 2005).

———, "The Political Ecology of War: Natural Resources and Armed Conflicts," *Political Geography* 20, no. 5 (2001): 561–584.

LeClercq, Hugues, "Le jeu des intérêts miniers dans le conflit congolais," paper prepared for the seminar "The Internal and Regional Dynamics of the Congo Crisis in 1999," Conflict Prevention Network, Brussels, January 5–6, 1999.

Lemarchand, René, "Genocide in the Great Lakes: Which Genocide? Whose Genocide," *African Studies Review* 41, no. 1 (1998): 3–16.

Licklider, Roy, "The Consequences of Negotiated Settlements in Civil Wars, 1945–1993," *American Political Science Review* 89, no. 3 (1995): 681–690.

Longman, Timothy, "The Complex Reasons for Rwanda's Engagement in Congo." In John F. Clark, ed., *The African Stakes of the Congo War* (New York: Palgrave Macmillan, 2002).

Lyons, Terrence, "Transforming the Institutions of War: Postconflict Elections and the Reconstruction of Failed States." In Robert I. Rotberg, ed., *When States Fail: Causes and Consequences* (Princeton: Princeton University Press, 2003).

MacGaffey, Janet, with Vwakyanakazi Mukohya, *The Real Economy of Zaire: The Contribution of Smuggling and Other Unofficial Activities to National Wealth* (Philadelphia: University of Philadelphia Press, 1991).

———, *Entrepreneurs and Parasites* (Cambridge: Cambridge University Press, 1986).

Malone, David M., and Heiko Nitzschke, "Economic Agendas in Civil Wars: What We Know, What We Need to Know," Discussion Paper No. 2005/07, World Institute for Development Economics Research, April 2005.

Mamdani, Mahmood, *When Victims Become Killers: Colonialism, Nativism, and the Genocide in Rwanda* (Princeton: Princeton University Press, 2001).

Matisonn, John, "Zimbabwe Top Brass Have Vested Interests in the DRC War," *Saturday Star* (Johannesburg), April 1, 2000, p. 5.

Maton, Jef, "Congo 1997–1999: La guerre des minerais et la fin temporaire des espoirs" (manuscript, University of Ghent, May 1999).

Maynard, Kimberly, *Healing Communities in Conflict: International Assistance in Complex Emergencies* (New York: Columbia University Press, 1999).

Misser, François, "Fools Rush In . . . and Out?" *African Business*, March 1998, pp. 27–28.

Mwanasali, Musifiki, "The View from Below." In M. Berdal and D. M. Malone, eds., *Greed and Grievance: Economic Agendas in Civil Wars* (Boulder, Colo.: Lynne Rienner, 2000), pp. 137–153.

Mwaura, Ciru, "Lessons for Regional Conflict Management and Conflict Prevention" (manuscript, Oxfam Great Britain, 2004).

Mwaura, Ciru, and Susanne Schmeidl, eds., *Early Warning and Conflict Management in the Horn of Africa* (Lawrenceville, N.J.: Red Sea Press, 2002).

Nafziger, Wayne E., and Juha Auvinen, *Economic Development, Inequality, and War: Humanitarian Emergencies in Developing Countries* (Basingstoke, England: Palgrave Macmillan, 2003).

Nest, Michael, "The Evolution of a Fragmented State: The Case of the Democratic Republic of Congo," Ph.D. diss., New York University, May 2002.

———, "Ambitions, Profits and Loss: Zimbabwean Economic Involvement in the Democratic Republic of the Congo," *African Affairs* 100, no. 400 (2001): 469–490.

Office of the Facilitator for the Inter-Congolese Dialogue, Final Report of the OFICD (Gaborone: OFICD, 2003).

———, *Accord global et inclusif sur la transition en République démocratique du Congo* (Pretoria: OFICD, 2002).

———, *Communiqué final des travaux du pré-dialogue* (Gaborone: OFICD, 2001).

———, *Declaration of Fundamental Principles of the Inter-Congolese Political Negotiations* (Lusaka: OFICD, May 4, 2001).

———, *Draft Agenda of the Inter-Congolese Dialogue* (Gaborone: OFICD), 2001.

———, Lusaka Ceasefire Agreement, July 10, 1999.

Organization for Economic Cooperation and Development, *Geographical Distribution of Financial Flows to Aid Recipients* (Paris: Development Assistance Committee).

Osmani, S. O., "The Food Problem of Bangladesh." In Jean Drèze, Amartya Sen, and Athar Husain, eds., *The Political Economy of Hunger* (Oxford: Clarendon Press, 1995).

Oxford Analytica, "Congo-Kinshasa: Resource Sector Brings Political Risks,"

Daily Briefing, July 20, 2005, available at www.oxan.com.

Pole Institute, *Natural Resource Exploitation and Human Security in the Democratic Republic of Congo*, Seminar Report (London and Goma, DRC: Pole Institute, February 2004).

Pugh, Michael, "Postwar Political Economy in Bosnia and Herzegovina: The Spoils of Peace," *Global Governance* 8, no. 4 (2002): 467–482.

Pugh, Michael, and Neil Cooper, with Jonathan Goodhand, *War Economies in a Regional Context: Challenges of Transformation* (Boulder, Colo.: Lynne Rienner, 2004).

Raeymaekers, Tim, *Network War: An Introduction to Congo's Privatised War Economy* (Brussels: International Peace Information Service, 2002).

Raftopoulos, Paul, "Briefing: Zimbabwe's 2002 Presidential Election," *African Affairs* 101, no. 404 (2002): 413–426.

Rajasingham, Darini, "The Dangers of Devolution: The Hidden Economies of Armed Conflict." In Robert Rotberg, ed., *Creating Peace in Sri Lanka* (Washington, D.C.: Brookings Institution Press, 1999).

Reno, William, *Warlord Politics and African States* (Boulder, Colo.: Lynne Rienner, 1998).

———, "Sovereignty and Personal Rule in Zaire," *African Studies Quarterly* 1, no. 3 (1997), available at www.clas.ufl.edu/africa/asq/v1/3/4.html.

Réseau Européen Congo, *Bulletin No. 7* (July 2001).

Ross, Michael L., "How Does Natural Resource Wealth Influence Civil War? Evidence from 13 Cases," *International Organization* 58, no. 1 (2004): 35–67.

———, "Oil, Drugs, and Diamonds: The Varying Roles of Natural Resources in Civil War." In Karen Ballentine and Jake Sherman, eds., *The Political Economy of Armed Conflict: Beyond Greed and Grievance* (Boulder, Colo. Lynne Rienner, 2003).

———, "Booty Futures: Africa's Civil Wars and the Futures Market for Natural Resources," paper presented at the American Political Science Association annual conference, 2002.

Rwanda, Government of, "Reaction of the Government of Rwanda to the Report of the Panel of Experts on the Illegal Exploitation of Natural Resources and Other Forms of Wealth of the Democratic Republic of Congo," Kigali, August 26, 2001, available at www.rwanda1.com/government/04_22_01news_Response_To_UN_Report.htm.

Sachs, Jeffrey D., and Andrew M. Warner, "The Curse of Natural Resources," *European Economic Review* 45 (2001): 827–838.

Samset, Ingrid, "Conflict of Interests or Interests in Conflict? Diamonds and War in the DRC," *Review of African Political Economy* 29, no. 93/94 (2002): 463–480.

Schatzberg, Michael G., *Mobutu or Chaos? The United States and Zaire, 1960–1990* (Philadelphia: University Press of America, 1991).

———, *Politics and Class in Zaire: Bureaucracy, Business, and Beer in Lisala* (New York: Africana Publishing Company, 1980).

Sen, Amartya K., *Poverty and Famines* (Oxford: Clarendon Press, 1981).

Shearer, David, "Africa's Great War," *Survival* 41, no. 2 (summer 1999).

Sherman, Jake, "Burma: Lessons from the Cease-Fires." In Karen Ballentine and Jake Sherman, eds., *The Political Economy of Armed Conflict: Beyond Greed and Grievance* (Boulder, Colo.: Lynne Rienner, 2003).

South African Broadcasting Corporation, "Congo Replaces 11 Ministers in Government Shuffle," January 4, 2005, available at www.sabc.gov.za.

Southern African Development Commission, Declaration and Treaty of the SADC Charter, 1992.

Spear, Joanna, "Disarmament and Demobilization." In Stephen J. Stedman, Donald Rothchild, and Elizabeth M. Cousens, eds., *Ending Civil Wars: The Implementation of Peace Agreements* (Boulder, Colo.: Lynne Rienner, 2002).

Standard, The (Harare), "ZDF Chief in DRC Mining Ventures," September 26–October 2, 1999, p. 1.

Stanley, William, *The Protection Racket State: Elite Politics, Military Extortion, and Civil War in El Salvador* (Philadelphia: Temple University Press, 1996).

Stedman, Stephen J., "Implementing Peace Agreements in Civil Wars: Lessons and Recommendations for Policy Makers" (New York: International Peace Academy, May 2001).

Stephen J. Stedman, Donald Rothchild, and Elizabeth M. Cousens, eds., *Ending Civil Wars: The Implementation of Peace Agreements* (Boulder, Colo.: Lynne Rienner, 2002).

Stewart, Frances, "Horizontal Inequalities as a Source of Conflict." In F. Osler Hampson and D. M. Malone, eds., *From Reaction to Conflict Prevention: Opportunities for the UN System* (Boulder, Colo.: Lynne Rienner, 2002), pp. 105–136.

Tegera, Aloys, *Nord-Kivu: Une rebellion dans la rebellion?* (Goma, DRC: Pole Institute, March 2003).

———, *Grands Lacs africains et perspective* (Goma, DRC: Pole Institute, October 4, 2002).

Tegera, Aloys, Sofia Mikolo, and Dominic Johnson, *The Coltan Phenomenon: How a Rare Mineral Has Changed the Life of the Population of War-Torn North Kivu Province in the East of the DRC* (Goma, DRC: Pole Institute, 2002).

Tull, Denis M., "A Reconfiguration of Political Order? The State of the State in North Kivu (DR Congo)," *African Affairs* 102, no. 408 (2003): 429–446.

Turner, Thomas, "Angola's Role in the Congo War." In John F. Clark, ed., *The African Stakes of the Congo War* (New York: Palgrave Macmillan, 2002).

United Nations, *Sixteenth Report of the Secretary-General on the United Nations Organization Mission in the DRC,* S/2004/1034, December 31, 2004, p. 5.

———, *Final Report of the Panel of Experts on the Illegal Exploitation of Natural Resources and Other Forms of Wealth of the Democratic Republic of Congo* (New York: UN, October 2002).

———, *Addendum to the Report of the Panel of Experts on the Illegal Exploitation of Natural Resources and Other Forms of Wealth of the Democratic Republic of Congo* (New York: UN, November 2001).

———, *Report of the Panel of Experts on the Illegal Exploitation of Natural Resources and Other Forms of Wealth of the Democratic Republic of the*

Congo (New York: UN, April 2001).

United Nations Development Programme, *Harnessing Institutional Capacities in Support of the Disarmament, Demobilization, and Reintegration of Former Combatants*, paper prepared by the Executive Committee on Humanitarian Assistance's Working Group on Disarmament, Demobilization, and Reintegration (New York: UN, 2000).

United Nations Office for the Coordination of Humanitarian Affairs–Integrated Regional Information Networks, "DRC: Talks on Transitional Government Stall over Army" (Geneva: OCHA, July 9, 2002).

United States Committee for Refugees, *World Refugee Survey* (Washington, D.C.: Immigration and Refugee Services of America, 1994).

United States Geological Survey, *Minerals Yearbook* (Washington D.C.: U.S. Bureau of Mines, 1991).

Van Acker, Frank, and Koen Vlassenroot, "Les 'Maï-Maï' et les functions de la violence milicienne dans l'est du Congo," *Politique Africaine,* no. 84 (December 2001): 103–116.

———, "Youth and Conflict in Kivu: Komona Clair," *Journal of Humanitarian Affairs* (2000), available at http://222.jha.ac/greatlakes/b004.htm.

Viane, L., "L'Organisation politique des Bahunde," *Kongo Oversee* 18 (1952).

Vick, Karl, "In the Waging of Congo's Wars, Vital Ore Plays Crucial Role," *International Herald Tribune*, March 20, 2001.

Vlassenroot, Koen, and Hans Romkema, "The Emergence of a New Order? Resources and War in Eastern Congo," *Journal of Humanitarian Assistance*, available online at www.jha.ac/articles/a111.htm.

Wagner, Robert H., "The Causes of Peace." In Roy Licklider, ed., *Stopping the Killing* (New York: New York University Press, 1993).

Weinstein, Jeremy M., "Africa's 'Scramble for Africa': Lessons of a Continental War," *World Policy Journal* (summer 2000): 11–20.

Whitman, Shelley, "Balancing Act: An Insider's View of the Inter-Congolese Dialogue," *African Studies Review* 12, no. 4 (2003): 133–135.

Willame, Jean-Claude, *Banyarwanda et Banyamulenge: Violences ethniques et gestion de l'identitaire au Kivu* (Brussels: Institut africain–CEDAF; Paris: L'Harmattan, 1997).

———, *Zaire: Predicament and Prospects* (New York: Minority Rights Group, 1997).

Wolters, Stephanie, "Continuing Instability in the Kivus: Testing the DRC Transition to the Limit," Occasional Paper No. 94 (Pretoria: Institute of Strategic Studies, 2004).

World Bank, DRC country page, http://web.worldbank.org, accessed March 20, 2005.

———, *Transitional Support Strategy for the Democratic Republic of the Congo* (Washington, D.C.: International Development Association, January 2004).

Young, Crawford, *Politics in the Congo: Decolonization and Independence* (Princeton: Princeton University Press, 1965).

Young, Crawford, and Thomas Turner, *The Rise and Decline of the Zairian State* (Madison: University of Wisconsin Press, 1985).

Index

Acquired Immune Deficiency Syndrome (AIDS), 109
Acquirement problem, 101
Addis Ababa talks, 74
Adjustment programs, 108, 121–122
Afghanistan, 19, 35, 42
African regional institutions, 133–134
African Union (AU), 76, 89, 133–134
Agriculture: extension services, 33; food production, 101, 103–105, 111; violence and output reduction in, 34–35
All-Inclusive Agreement on the Transition in the Democratic Republic of Congo (December 2002), 76
Alliance des Forces Démocratiques pour la Libération du Congo-Zaire (AFDL), 23–25, 89
Allied Democratic Forces (ADF) (Uganda), 70
Anglo-American plc, 42
Angola: competition over natural resources in, 11; entry into Congo War, 25–26, 39; as failed state, 19; institutional legacies, 107; Mobutu overthrow role of, 20, 23; natural resources as motive for war in, 131; oil ventures with DRC, 50–51; peace accord in DRC, 65; regional differences in economy of, 35, 42; roadblock commerce by troops of,

42; withdrawal of UNITA forces from DRC, 70
Annan, Kofi, 76
Armed conflict: civil wars as focus in analysis of, 11; entrepreneurial advantages to, 54; following DRC peace accords, 65–66; groups' motives for, 37, 39; local, 12, 32, 134; rebel groups violence toward civilians, 83; regional approach to, 133
Arms dealers, 41
Arslanian Frères, 46
Association for the Salvation of the Dialogue (ASD), 75
Atrocities, 35
Autochthonous groups, 20, 22

Ballentine, Karen, 130
Baluba (people), 23
Banks, 53
Banyamulenge, 21–22, 36–37, 102
Banyarwanda, 21–22, 36–37, 102
Belgium: appropriation of land in the Kivus, 21; as colonial power in Congo, 13, 17; in Congo's postindependence era, 18; DRC relations, 38; economic interests in DRC, 68, 93n10
Bemba, Jean-Pierre: as MLC leader, 25; as MLC president, 48; peace accords, 79; Sun City talks, 75; Uganda influence on, 82–83

War role for, 26; Mobutu support for, 23; Namibia attacks by, 59*n25;* Rwanda/Uganda visits by leaders of, 39; withdrawal from DRC of, 70
Union des Patriotes Congolais, 78
Union pour la Démocratie et le Progrès Social (UDPS), 75
United Kingdom, 69, 87, 91, 97*n56*
United Nations Children's Fund (UNICEF), 108, 115
United Nations Development Programme (UNDP), 100, 108, 115–116
United Nations High Commissioner for Refugees (UNHCR), 20
United Nations Observer Mission to the DRC (MONUC): cease fire in Orientale province, 83; DDRRR programs, 113–115, 126*n45;* establishment of, 85; failure to disarm Hutu militias, 130; rebel occupation of Bukavu, 66; reconstruction programs of, 100, 108; successes and failures of, 132; transitional government of DRC, 76; Western role in DRC and, 68
United Nations Panel of Experts: addendum to reports on resource exploitation, 74; combatants response to reports of, 69; effects of reports of, 132–133; establishment of, 72, 84–86; extortion, 51–52, 56; failure of, 88–89; foreign economic interests in DRC, 44, 51–53
United Nations Security Council (UNSC): Resolution 1341 (2001), 113; Resolution 1492 (2003), 115; Western powers role in, 68, 85–88
United States: as coltan processor, 37; DRC relations, 38; economic interests in DRC, 68–69; French Great Lakes role and, 97*n56;* UN Panel of

Experts, 91; view of Lumumba government, 18
Université de Lubumbashi, 19

Van Acker, Frank, 135
Victoria Group, 48
Vlassenroot, Koen, 135

Waged labor, 101–102
Wages, 101
Wamba, Wamba dia, 82, 94*n17*
War economy legacies, 101–108
Warlords, 20, 42
West Nile Bank Front (WNBF), 70
Widows, 115
Women as workers, 104
World Bank: DDRRR, 113; DRC mining code, 46, 117; future of DRC, 99; Kabila government antipathy toward, 38; reconstruction programs of, 100, 108–109, 112
World Bank Group, 118
World Health Organization (WHO), 108

Zaire. *See* Congo, Democratic Republic of
Zambia, 29*n21,* 67, 70
Zimbabwe: copper production role of, 42, 50; diamond smuggling role of, 41; DRC debt to, 84; economic effect of Congo War on, 40–41; entry into Congo War, 25; export of commodities from DRC, 35; motives for entering conflict, 39, 69; post–peace accord strategy in DRC, 84; private entrepreneurs from, 50, 57*n5,* 84; role in production of diamonds, 38, 43, 50; SADC role of, 39–40
Zimbabwe African National Union–Patriotic Front (ZANU-PF), 50
Zimbabwe Defence Forces (ZDF), 25–26; diamond mining, 45
ZimTrade, 41

About This Publication

Despite the prominent role that competition over natural resources has played in some of Africa's most intractable conflicts, little research has been devoted to what the economic dimensions of armed conflict mean for peace operations and efforts to reconstruct war-torn states. Redressing this gap, this book analyzes the challenges that the war economy posed, and continues to pose, for policymakers and practitioners in the Democratic Republic of Congo.

The authors first trace the historical role of natural resource exploitation in shaping economic development and governance in Zaire (now the DRC). Then turning to the 1998–2004 period, they assess how economic interests shaped both the peace process and the belligerents' attitudes toward resolution of the violent conflict that wracked the country. They also address the impact of the war economy on postwar reconstruction and identify strategies for more effective approaches to resolving—and even preventing—further economically driven civil wars.

Michael Nest is a consultant, focusing on political and social issues related to the extraction of natural resources. His recent projects include studies of Zimbabwean economic involvement in the DRC and of the challenges of "consent agreements" between mining companies and communities consenting to minerals activities on their lands. **François Grignon** is head of the UN Mission's Conflict and Prevention Unit in the DRC. He served previously as deputy director of the French Institute for Research in Africa (IFRA) and as Central Africa project director for the International Crisis Group's Nairobi office. **Emizet F. Kisangani** is an associate professor of political science at Kansas State University. He is author of *Zaire After Mobutu: A Case of a Humanitarian Emergency* and is currently working on a book titled *State Formation/State Disintegration: A Cycle of Symbolism, Capital Accumulation, and Elite Coalition in Congo.*

The International Peace Academy

The International Peace Academy (IPA) is an independent, international institution dedicated to promoting the prevention and settlement of armed conflicts between and within states through policy research and development.

Founded in 1970, the IPA has built an extensive portfolio of activities in fulfillment of its mission:

- Symposiums, workshops, and other forums that facilitate strategic thinking, policy development, and organizational innovation within international organizations.
- Policy research on multilateral efforts to prevent, mitigate, or rebuild after armed conflict.
- Research, consultations, and technical assistance to support capacities for peacemaking, peacekeeping, and peacebuilding in Africa.
- Professional-development seminars for political, development, military, humanitarian, and nongovernmental personnel involved in peacekeeping and conflict resolution.
- Facilitation in conflict situations where its experience, credibility, and independence can complement official peace efforts.
- Outreach to build public awareness on issues related to peace and security, multilateralism, and the United Nations.

The IPA works closely with the United Nations, regional and other international organizations, governments, and nongovernmental organizations, as well as with parties to conflicts in selected cases. Its efforts are enhanced by its ability to draw on a worldwide network of government and business leaders, scholars, diplomats, military officers, and leaders of civil society.

The IPA is a nonprofit organization governed by an international Board of Directors. The organization is funded by generous donations from governments, major philanthropic foundations, and corporate donors, as well as contributions from individuals and its Board members.

International Peace Academy Publications

Available from Lynne Rienner Publishers, 1800 30th Street, Boulder, Colorado 80301 (303-444-6684), www.rienner.com.

Kashmir: New Voices, New Approaches, edited by Waheguru Pal Singh Sidhu, Bushra Asif, and Cyrus Samii (2006)

The Democratic Republic of Congo: Economic Dimensions of War and Peace, Michael Nest, with François Grignon and Emizet F. Kisangani (2006)

East Africa and the Horn: Confronting Challenges to Good Governance, edited by Dorina A. Bekoe (2006)

Profiting from Peace: Managing the Resource Dimensions of Civil War, edited by Karen Ballentine and Heiko Nitzschke (2005)

Western Sahara: Anatomy of a Stalemate, Erik Jensen (2005)

Exploring Subregional Conflict: Opportunities for Conflict Prevention, edited by Chandra Lekha Sriram and Zoe Nielsen (2004)

West Africa's Security Challenges: Building Peace in a Troubled Region, edited by Adekeye Adebajo and Ismail Rashid (2004)

War Economies in a Regional Context: Challenges of Transformation, Michael Pugh and Neil Cooper, with Jonathan Goodhand (2004)

The UN Security Council: From the Cold War to the Twenty-First Century, edited by David M. Malone (2004)

The United Nations and Regional Security: Europe and Beyond, edited by Michael Pugh and Waheguru Pal Singh Sidhu (2003)

The Political Economy of Armed Conflict: Beyond Greed and Grievance, edited by Karen Ballentine and Jake Sherman (2003)

From Promise to Practice: Strengthening UN Capacities for the

Prevention of Violent Conflict, edited by Chandra Lekha Sriram and Karin Wermester (2003)

The Chittagong Hill Tracts, Bangladesh: On the Difficult Road to Peace, Amena Mohsin (2003)

Peacekeeping in East Timor: The Path to Independence, Michael G. Smith, with Moreen Dee (2003)

From Cape to Congo: Southern Africa's Evolving Security Challenges, edited by Mwesiga Baregu and Christopher Landsberg (2003)

Ending Civil Wars: The Implementation of Peace Agreements, edited by Stephen John Stedman, Donald Rothchild, and Elizabeth M. Cousens (2002)

Sanctions and the Search for Security: Challenges to UN Action, David Cortright and George A. Lopez, with Linda Gerber (2002)

Ecuador vs. Peru: Peacemaking Amid Rivalry, Monica Herz and João Pontes Nogueira (2002)

Liberia's Civil War: Nigeria, ECOMOG, and Regional Security in West Africa, Adekeye Adebajo (2002)

Building Peace in West Africa: Liberia, Sierra Leone, and Guinea-Bissau, Adekeye Adebajo (2002)

Kosovo: An Unfinished Peace, William G. O'Neill (2002)

From Reaction to Conflict Prevention: Opportunities for the UN System, edited by Fen Osler Hampson and David M. Malone (2002)

Peacemaking in Rwanda: The Dynamics of Failure, Bruce D. Jones (2001)

Self-Determination in East Timor: The United Nations, the Ballot, and International Intervention, Ian Martin (2001)

Civilians in War, edited by Simon Chesterman (2001)

Toward Peace in Bosnia: Implementing the Dayton Accords, Elizabeth M. Cousens and Charles K. Cater (2001)

Sierra Leone: Diamonds and the Struggle for Democracy, John L. Hirsch (2001)

Peacebuilding as Politics: Cultivating Peace in Fragile Societies, edited by Elizabeth M. Cousens and Chetan Kumar (2001)

The Sanctions Decade: Assessing UN Strategies in the 1990s, David Cortright and George A. Lopez (2000)

Greed and Grievance: Economic Agendas in Civil War, edited by Mats Berdal and David M. Malone (2000)

Building Peace in Haiti, Chetan Kumar (1998)

Rights and Reconciliation: UN Strategies in El Salvador, Ian Johnstone (1995)